A Gradual Grace

Christina Marigold Houen

A Gradual Grace
The final memoir

For my children,
who taught me how to love and let go,
and love again

A Gradual Grace: The final memoir
ISBN 978 1 76109 555 9
Copyright © text Christina Marigold Houen 2023
Cover image: *Kintsugi*, by Stuart Cussons

First published 2023 by
Ginninderra Press
PO Box 3461 Port Adelaide 5015
www.ginninderrapress.com.au

Farther in summer than the birds,
Pathetic from the grass,
A minor nation celebrates
Its unobtrusive mass.

No ordinance is seen,
So gradual the grace,
A pensive custom it becomes,
Enlarging loneliness.

– Emily Dickinson

One

He was dying. My daughters were in Perth with him, witnessing his last hours as he lay in a coma. My daughters, whom he stole from me when they were little. He was a workaholic, building a world reputation as a computer scientist, more away than he was at home.

Yet, in his old age, as he became alcoholic and diabetic, and began to dement, they forgave him. Sophia, the eldest, looked after him for the last three and a half years after his third wife died.

Nearly two decades earlier, when I was fifty-nine, I went back to university and began to write my story. It was then that I got in touch with my anger. I refused to keep up the charade I had maintained for their sakes throughout the years – that he and I were friends. I refused to see him or have anything more to do with him. But in the last few years, he somehow got hold of my phone number and would ring me, often late at night, and want to talk.

Each time, he'd ask the same questions. 'Are you with anyone now? What went wrong?'

To the latter, I'd reply, 'Robert, I don't think there's any point in going over what happened. We both made mistakes. We made choices that had irreversible consequences. Our daughters have lived with that and are grown up.'

I asked Sophia to delete my number from his phone. I knew he had a fantasy that I would return to him.

That Saturday morning, when I knew he was dying, I woke after a dream that was unlike any I've ever had. He came to me, desirous, and I felt desire for him such as I never felt when we were together.

'All right,' I said, 'let's be together one last time, and then we can forgive each other and let go.'

And so we did.

Later that day, I got the news he had died, still in a coma. I felt little.

Next morning, I turned on my computer. An old man's voice, singing, came on. I hadn't opened any programs. I hadn't used Spotify for a couple of weeks and certainly hadn't listened to that song, which I vaguely remembered from the film many years before. Where was it coming from? I tracked the song and found a YouTube video of Burt Bacharach singing 'Alfie'. That was the voice I'd heard. I listened to the song and looked up the lyrics.

Alfie was nothing until he could find the love that he'd missed. Perhaps that was what Robert was searching for in those last days. He realised he'd been cruel because only fools are kind. He believed that he had to be strong and powerful because others would take advantage of him. He'd been bullied as a child because he was bright, small, different. So he had to push himself to prove his worth, to become successful, to make a world reputation in his field, to acquire wealth. If others got hurt along the way, they were to blame for their folly. If they hurt him, he would take revenge. But his life, after all his ambitious striving and self-promotion and sacrifice of others, had come to nothing.

It hit me. He was trying to apologise to me. Now he'd left his body, he could see that he'd been cruel to me and to his daughters, keeping them from me as they were growing up, subjecting them to an abusive stepfamily, trying to shape them to his will. He wanted my forgiveness. And as I had dreamt it, yet differently, slowly, I began to release him, I began to forgive him. Not all at once, but in stages. Which means I was also able to forgive myself for the choices that separated my daughters from me.

Maybe I'm not finished yet, as I witness things still happening in my daughter's lives. How many times do I need to forgive him, forgive myself? Or is it simply that he is no longer relevant? Whatever wrong he did to us, we have had a lifetime to turn that wrong into a gift. This is a story of dark gifts that have been turned into gold. There are some still to turn in the alchemy of love.

Time and memory are coupled together. Time holds memory, but time is elusive and illusionary. The tenses of past, present and future create a sense of order and control. But life is not so straightforward. We think we live in the present and have laid the pattern for our future, but our past keeps intruding and often shapes the way we live our lives. Meditational arts teach us to be present, yet we find this so difficult.

My practice in this story is to review the past and relive it through the music of words, bringing the lessons that are embedded in it into my present reality. So that I do not keep repeating the patterns I was locked in. In this story, tense is fluid, time floats between past and present while we dream of our future. So I invite my reader to float free with me as I shift between now, then and perhaps.

Emily Dickinson, that wild, free spirit who led a tame, reclusive life, wrote poems and letters that startle and shock with their passion and asymmetry, their glimpses of a life lived aslant in an ordered, repressed, hierarchical household. The words woven into her poems strike black notes that are sharp, sometimes flat, and make one wonder about the hidden meaning. Ordinance, for instance, from the Latin *ordinare*, to put in order, is absent from the minor mass the crickets sing. The loneliness of their music reflects the loneliness of a woman trapped in a patriarchal world, unable to live the asymmetrical life she wants to live. The music is subversive in its quiet, unobtrusive celebration of the end of summer. My words join in this mass and celebrate the triumph of four women's lives over the ordinance that sought to control and suppress them.

Sometimes, this Hecate, this wild, triple goddess, complies and obeys. Sometimes, she resists and rebels. Sometimes, she is broken.

Demeter had a daughter by Zeus, the ruler of heaven. Her beautiful, white-armed daughter, Persephone, played with the other goddesses on Mount Aetna in Sicily, where all the flowers of mountain, wood and field grew. One day, Persephone saw a narcissus, sister of the daffodil.

It was shining like yellow gold and had a sweet, delicate perfume. Persephone bent over and plucked it, but when she did, a hole opened up in the ground and she fell through. The other goddesses ran to tell Demeter what had happened. The world went dark, the sun was veiled. She neglected her duties as goddess of fertility and fruitfulness and the crops failed and fruit did not form on the trees. She had not taught anyone else the secrets of how to make the earth yield food, so people got very hungry.

Hecate, the triple-formed goddess, walked by her sister Demeter's side, bearing a torch that never went out. Demeter wandered for nine days and nights searching for her lost girl. Nine days in world time was nine months, nine years, nine lives in heart time.

Demeter the mother is the spirit of my incarnation in this lifetime and Hecate is my soul sister, though I lost not one daughter but three. Our reunions in their childhood were always regulated and limited – ordered – by their father, the cruel winter king who kept them as close as he could for his own power and gratification and allowed them to be bullied and abused by their stepfamily.

Hecate is Demeter's companion in her search for her lost daughters. She bears the torch that lights the path and in her liminal magic is able to cross thresholds and enter the underworld of winter, death and imprisonment without being destroyed. She is a protector, but she is also dangerous and can use her powers as much for destruction as for deliverance. If angered, she becomes a destroyer. Demeter is aware of Hecate's three-sidedness and seeks to keep her balance by staying centred in her heart and her motherhood. Being a mother is her purpose in life and the source of love and compassion and creativity.

There is no ordinance for this song, no predictability. Just when you think the song is finished, it starts again.

So now, I tell the story of the enlargement of loneliness in my life and my gradual, unseen celebration of the dark gifts I was given, an unobtrusive mass to life and love.

Two

At thirty-two when I lost my daughters, I began the long journey of learning to live separately from them, of witnessing them grow up without my mothering except in short-dated bundles, of discovering they were being abused by their stepfamily and not being able to intervene, of trying to find a reason for living, a way of being on my own. I gradually lost the hard rock in my stomach, the lump of anger and grief and regret, and the empty ache in my heart, and found a way of living that had some meaning. But it took many years, half a lifetime.

In the early years after I lost them, I became a mental health nurse and found some worth and purpose in helping others whose lives were more broken than mine.

But always my heart felt empty, except for when the girls were with me, and even then, I ached underneath the fun and joy that we shared, because I knew we would have to part again.

Once, when I was doing general nursing training, in 'block', when we had chunks of theory thrown at us, I lay outside on the grass at break time with a friend. With the cicadas shrilling in the trees and the crickets' quieter, rhythmic trilling in the grass, we chatted idly about our lives.

She talked of what she wanted to do when she'd finished training. 'What about you, Anna?'

'Oh, you know what?' I said, as I riffled my fingers through the grass and gazed up at the fluffy white clouds drifting across the late summer sky, 'I have no idea. I don't really care what I do. Sometimes I wish I could leave this life and come back into another life, one that has more meaning for me.'

My friend was religious. 'Oh,' she said in a shocked tone, 'don't you believe in God? "To everything there is a season, A time for every purpose under heaven."'

'No, Olive, I don't. Not a personal god, anyway. One day, I might find out what my life has been about. I thought it was about finding someone who'd love me as an equal, who'd see me as I am, and having children with him, building a life together. Now, I'm a mother without my children, and I'm alone. They have to grow up without me, in a family where they're not safe.'

'Why can't you get custody?' Olive raised her head and rested her chin on her elbow as she gazed at me.

'Because he has possession, he has a profession, he has a house, and I'm a student nurse on a low income. I rent, and can't provide for them as he does. And because they would have to go to court and testify that they are being cruelly treated. He refuses to acknowledge that there's a problem and turns a blind eye. And he has told them that if they leave him, he will die. So they're afraid to go.'

'Oh. I see.' She dropped her eyes and sank back on the grass.

The bell rang, and we got up and went back into class.

The afternoon session was taken up by a guest presenter. The topic, drug and alcohol counselling.

The presenter was in his early forties, with long hair tied back in a ponytail, eyes veiled by smoke-tinted glasses, unsmiling. He talked to us about how he counselled his clients, focusing not on their addictions but on the underlying causes. 'It always goes back to early childhood,' he said, taking off his glasses and fixing me with an intense gaze. 'A child's first seven years shape the rest of their life. If they are not kept safe, if they are not loved, they will grow up with a craving for what they lost or never knew. That is the seat of all addiction.' He shifted his gaze to the guy sitting next to me, who was fiddling with his biro and looking down at an empty notepad. 'So, in my work, I help them to get in touch with that small, hungry being that felt left out, not noticed, or that was not kept safe.'

I felt he could see inside me, into my hungry heart. At the end of the session, he put a few of his business cards on the table and invited us to contact him if we wanted to talk about any of the issues he'd raised for us.

I made an appointment to see him at his rooms in a nearby suburb. I saw him about three times, but each time, I came away feeling empty and invisible. I would sit there for an hour, trying to talk about the things in my life I could not change. He sat there with his gaze fixed on me, saying little. If I fell silent, he sat silent too, waiting for me to speak again.

Halfway through the third session, I said, 'I'm just going through the motions. I don't really care what I do. I'm passing time.'

He gazed back at me and said nothing.

I struck my chest with my right hand and said, 'In my heart, here, it's empty.'

He sat silent.

I stood up and said, 'I won't come back to see you. I'm not getting anything out of these sessions.'

I can't remember what he said as I picked up my bag and pushed my chair in, but he implied that it was I who had failed, not him.

I went on with my training, moving from ward to ward. Some were worse than others. The worst one for me was Accident and Emergency. I was terrified of all the equipment and the prospect of having to resuscitate someone or help deal with serious injuries.

One night, as I was assisting with a woman who'd taken an overdose and was having her stomach pumped, the sister in charge said to me, 'Look, nurse, you're not much help here. The man in the next cubicle has a broken femur. He's had morphine for pain, the most we can give him, but he's still complaining. Can you go and sit with him and try to distract him?'

He was lying on the narrow bed, upper leg splinted, intravenous infusion dripping into the canula in his arm. He was sweating, his upper body twisting, eyes squeezed shut, mouth pulled back in a grimace, moaning. I sat beside him and introduced myself. He opened his eyes and looked at me, then closed them again.

'Can I hold your hand?' I said.

He opened his clenched, sweaty fist and I laid my hand across his palm.

'Tell me what's on your mind.'

For the next hour, he talked to me about the pain, what he remembered of his accident, what his worries and fears were. I kept my eyes on his face, which gradually relaxed, and his words slowed down, with long pauses. His breathing became softer and slower until he fell asleep. His fingers were still curled around mine, so I left my hand there, shifting my position from time to time to ease my back.

It was getting light, and the busy sounds and voices that signalled change of shift told me I would soon be released.

The sister came into the cubicle, checked his pulse, and smiled at me. 'Well, nurse, you can let go of his hand now. You've done well. I don't think you'll make an A and E nurse, but clearly, you're good with people.'

Three

I moved from the little terrace house my cousin and I rented in Rozelle to Cremorne Point. There, we shared the ground floor of an old two-storey house that was falling apart at the seams. It was in a prime spot for development, bordering the reserve that stretched along the edge of the harbour. From upstairs, there was a view of the harbour and beyond to the city. The owner wanted to sell it, but there were two old ladies living upstairs, one in her nineties, and she refused to move. Under the tenancy laws, he had to wait until she either died or went into care.

My girls visited me twice a year, a fortnight each time. Their father had brought them back from the United States to Australia with the extended family when Sophia was ten, Caitlin eight and Penelope five. He took a job in Melbourne as foundation chair of the university's department of computer science, so I could only see them on their allotted holidays with me.

Penelope's tenth birthday was coming up in the new year while they were with me, and her sisters and I decided to make it a surprise Paddington Bear party. Penelope had a passion for Paddington. She longed for a big one, but I couldn't afford that, so I bought a small one. Caitlin and Sophia set about making a house for Paddington to live in, with Madame Cholet as his wife. She was the feisty chef of the burrow inhabited by their favourite TV cartoon characters, the Wombles. An unlikely match, but it suited their story. They worked on Paddington's house while I took Penelope out for swimming lessons. I'd discovered she was still dog-paddling – Kate, her stepmother, had refused to take her to lessons as a punishment for some misdemeanour.

The older girls made a cardboard house with two levels and set up the kitchen, dining room and an upstairs bedroom, furnished with matchboxes glued together and covered with scraps of bright floral and striped fabric that one of the old ladies upstairs gave them from her sewing basket. At night, when the girls were asleep, I made a chocolate cake with two layers and iced it. Next morning, the day of her birthday, I took Penelope out for her last swimming lesson, and the girls decorated the cake with miniature Paddington, Madame Cholet and some marzipan flowers. When we came home, they had the Paddington mansion furnished and, as we walked into the living room, they put on the album I'd bought, with Bernard Cribbins singing 'A Bear Called Paddington'. They'd lit the candles on the cake, in pride of place on the coffee table where Paddington's house stood. We sang along and clapped at the end, and Penelope blew the candles out. My present for her was the latest Paddington Bear book, *Paddington Takes the Test*. Sophia and Caitlin gave her a PB card game and a board game.

As she snuggled down on the mattress near her sisters that night, she put her arms around my neck and whispered, 'Mama, this is the best birthday I've ever had!'

Four

That autumn, I had a letter from Michael. He and his wife, an Australian couple, had been friends with Robert and me when we lived in England. They got to know us after they rented our house on the Atomic Energy Authority estate when Robert took a sabbatical at Boulder University in Colorado. When we returned, they'd bought a house on the estate, and were friends with many people we knew. They returned to Perth after Robert and I separated. Now, Michael said in his letter, he and his wife were divorced and he was taking a job with a company that wanted him to do some training in Sydney. Could we meet for dinner?

That meal, a spicy Korean barbecue with plenty of good red wine and shared memories and heartaches, morphed into a weekend spent together, shopping in the city, browsing through bookshops, getting the ferry to Taronga Zoo. We roamed hand in hand around the zoo, talking to the animals. Michael made up little stories about many of them and made me laugh. Evening was falling, and we decided to walk back to Cremorne Point. We threaded our way home, sharing stories of our life in England and the ups and downs of our marriages and break-ups, our dreams and our losses. By the time we got to my place, we were contemplating a future together.

When Michael went back to Perth, we wrote to each other a couple of times a week, and he would ring me when he could. He had moved back to live with his parents, as his wife was still living in the big house with all the antique furniture she'd brought out from England. He'd left with only his clothes and a couple of blankets. He had two daughters: one in her early twenties was living with her boyfriend, and the younger one was doing the higher school certificate, still living with her mother.

Michael didn't want his parents to know we were considering living together. I found it odd and asked him why.

'Oh, Mum would think it's too soon after Camilla and I broke up. And I think she likes having me back home. I don't want to tell her yet.'

He would ring me from a phone box near his parents' place. The timing of the calls was erratic. When I was doing shift work, I would often get home at ten at night, and have to get up at five next morning to go to an early shift. By the time I'd wound down and closed my eyes, I might have five to six hours at best. Sometimes, he would ring me after I'd drifted off to sleep. I'd struggle out of bed into the living room and talk for a while, then back to bed. A few times, I asked him not to ring me late at night.

When the girls came for their mid-year visit to me, I told them about Michael and how I might be going to live with him in Perth.

'But Mama, why can't he come and live with you here?' Sophia asked. 'If you go to Perth, will we still be able to visit you?'

'Of course, darling. Nothing will stop me seeing you.'

'But what about Nanna? We won't be able to see her! She'll miss you and us so much! And we won't have fun times with Uncle David and Aunty Jo.'

'Oh, I know. It's hard. I'm not going to rush into this. I'll think about it carefully before I make a decision.'

My brother David and his wife Jo lived next door to Mum in the main part of the house. Mum had a comfortable two-bedroom granny flat in a lovely harbourside suburb, with friendly neighbours. When my girls were visiting, she would take us into the city on the ferry and to lunch in posh restaurants like the Summit, a revolving restaurant at the top of Australia Square. She would save her silver coins, a jarful for each granddaughter, so they had spending money for treats.

When my father left, Mum wouldn't let David come home and help her run the farm.

He told me, a few years before he died, that she'd said, 'No, you're not destined to be a farmer. You'll be a city lawyer. You must stay in Sydney and finish your law degree.' He said he knew that if he had come back, my life would have been very different.

I cried when he told me. I lost my childhood when my father left. I had to grow up overnight and try to fill some of the empty space in our life and in her heart.

Twenty-five years later, I did what my father had done, but in reverse. I walked away and left my daughters with their father. But my dad left of his own accord and against Mum's will, whereas Robert forced me to leave and threatened murder and suicide if I took the girls from him.

David and Jo were shocked when I returned to Sydney in distress after I'd left them. But David found me a lawyer and, like Mum, they were loyal and supportive through those hard years.

Whenever the girls visited me, we'd have lovely times there. The girls would swim and play in the pool, and we'd share a meal and play word games round the table, and afterwards, Grandma's Suitcase. I don't know if we made this game up. It went like this. Jo would provide two old suitcases filled with clothes from a dress-up box. We'd form two teams, and the leader of each team would have to dress as fast as possible, run up to the goal and back, undress, and the next team member would do the same. The girls and I would end up rolling on the carpet with laughter, especially when David, six feet tall, had to squeeze himself into Mum's old dresses and hobble along in Jo's pointy shoes, carrying suitcase and handbag.

The last morning of the girls' visit, Sophia looked at me with her head on one side and said, 'Mama, who were you talking to on the phone late last night?'

'I wasn't.'

Caitlin giggled and said, 'Yes, you were. I woke up too and I heard you.'

'What did I say?'

"'Yes, darling, I love you too.'"

'Oh, it must have been Michael. That's weird. I have no memory of it!'

But…how could I have got up, walked from the bedroom to the phone in the living room, had a conversation with him, then gone back to bed, and have no memory of it?

Next time he rang, I asked him if he'd rung me late that night.

'Yes, I went out for a late walk when the folks were asleep and found a phone box that had coins jammed in it, so I could make a free phone call. I couldn't resist.'

'Michael, please don't ring me late at night! It's a struggle getting enough sleep when I do shift work, and it bothers me that I have no memory of speaking to you. I've no idea what I said.'

'You didn't say much. Just that you love me.'

We'd write each other long letters; his were a mix of anecdotes of his life and poetic, passionate desire for me; mine were rambling stories of my life and my thoughts, snatches of songs I was listening to, bits from books I was reading. Our tastes in literature overlapped somewhat, though I found his a bit old-fashioned – G.K. Chesterton, E.M. Forster. In music, he was into Frank Sinatra and Bing Crosby and I was listening to the Moody Blues, Don McLean, the Allman Brothers, Santana – tastes I'd acquired when I started psych nursing and was introduced to an alternative world I hadn't known in my marriage.

I liked Michael's poetic, romantic soul and his gentle, intuitive nature, his funny ways that made me laugh, but I found his letters more interesting and exciting than our phone conversations. On the phone, he sounded flat, talking in a monotone with long pauses. I wondered if we really could connect as soulmates and lovers in a long-term relationship. The fact that he was staying with his parents bothered me. True, I had stayed with my mother when I was separated from the children but, as soon as I could, I got my own flat. Whereas Michael seemed to be living like he had as a young man before he was married, hiding his relationship with me from his parents, conforming to their quiet, domestic, boring life, and expressing his desires and dreams on paper to me.

He would turn forty-nine the following February, and I would be forty. Perhaps he was too old for me, a different generation. I knew nothing about his life in Perth, except that he was passionate about golf and had a job as a sales rep with a company that supplied chemicals and plastics to retailers. It sounded mundane, but he liked getting out and about and meeting different people. It was a change from his profession in pharmacy, which he'd entered at his parents' insistence although he wanted to be a journalist.

He had been offered a cadetship with the main Perth newspaper, but took his parents' advice and stuck to finishing his pharmacy degree. Ever since, he'd wanted to escape. In some ways, he said, he had liked it much better when he was in his twenties, when pharmacists made a lot of their own pills and potions. It had changed from a respected professional service to a shopkeeper's role, dispensing manufactured medications, toiletries, make-up and jewellery. In his soul, he was a storyteller, but he was trapped in a boring profession. He poured his poetic longings into his letters to me. I responded to the poetry and dreamed of a lover who would see me and love me as I am. But I feared giving up everything I had in Sydney for life in a faraway place with no friends but him, having to start all over again.

My general nursing training was a short course over two years. By the end of that year, I'd have done fifteen months of it, just another nine to go. I didn't like all the technical stuff, calculating dosages, learning to use equipment, changing dressings, taking physical observations. The friends I had were from my psych nursing days, and I found little to talk about to the other general trainees, who were mostly younger than me and thought that having a good time was going to a bar or a party and getting drunk, looking for a one-night stand at a night club or seeing the latest American movie. I couldn't imagine a career in a general hospital.

So why was I doing it? After I'd graduated in psych nursing, I took a job as a community mental health nurse on the northern beaches. But the clinic was a new service in an affluent area and there wasn't enough work to keep me busy. I had loved my training years, working in a busy psych hospital that was shifting away from the old regime of institutionalising patients. The psych training had covered medical and surgical nursing, but in a limited way, and there was a trend for general hospitals to open up psych wards, with a preference for staff with a double certificate. I thought getting a double certificate would give me more options.

When I had days off work, I'd go to the park and sit on the grassy bank looking out over the harbour, reading Michael's latest letter, writing back to him. I couldn't make up my mind whether to stay as I was and finish my training or go to Perth to join him. It was so far away, the other side of the continent, with desert in between.

I loved Sydney. I'd lived there since the last year of my schooling, through my student days, my marriage to Robert at twenty, then five more years until we went to live in England. When we returned eight years later and our marriage fell apart, I went back to Sydney and survived those seven years as a single woman without my children. My life wasn't happy, but I felt held by the city, the harbour, the rich, layered life of the inner city and suburbs, and by Mum, David and Jo. They'd seen me go through the worst days of my life and had always been there for me. How could I leave them, leave my Sydney, go to an unknown city, to a man I'd only spent one weekend with, whose family I didn't know, and be farther away than ever from my girls?

And yet, my life felt empty. My childhood dream of finding a man who would love me as an equal and not abandon me was still strong. My children had been the crown and comfort of my life throughout my empty marriage, and now they were my holiday daughters in small rations. I couldn't contemplate living the rest of my life without my own family. Could Michael and I make a family? Would he be a good stepfather to my daughters? He told me he loved children. Was that enough to go on?

Five

Perth… What can I say about it? I lived there for thirty-two years, and for a lot of that time I wanted to leave. It never felt like home to me. Physically, I found it flat, spread out, sandy and shallow. The ocean was a beautiful turquoise blue, unlike the green waters of Sydney Harbour and its ocean beaches. The sun rose and set on the wrong sides of the world. The newer suburbs stretched for miles, endless replicas of dull brick houses and the trendy new-wealthy mansions of concrete that take up the whole block.

Socially, like the soil it was on, Perth had fewer layers than Sydney. I thought it was shallow and materialistic. There was a thin layer of elites, descendants of the early settler families with inherited land and wealth and a sense of privilege and superiority, and there were the working poor, the middle classes of professionals and students, and the new rich, but I met few people I could share my interests and inner self with. In fact, in thirty-two years there, I made only one friendship that lasted.

Michael and I lived in a succession of cheap two-bedroom flats in small blocks. The nicest one was on the edge of Hyde Park in an inner-city suburb. There were two lakes, one with an island in the centre of it, inhabited by ducks, swans, coots and other smaller water birds, and turtles. On fine days, there would be several groups of older Italian men sitting on the benches, yarning, or playing boules on the grass. Families with little children came to picnic and barbecue. There was always life to watch…other people's lives, other people's families.

With no one but Michael, I felt lonely and isolated. During the week, we both worked. On Saturdays, he would set off mid-morning for his golf club, where he'd been a member all his life, and return home after dark, sometimes at eight or nine o'clock after the nineteenth hole. I would spend my Saturdays walking in the park, reading, watching other people's lives. I hated him spending the whole day at golf when we only had two days together. I was silently angry and resentful. His golfing friends bored me on the few occasions we went to a party, and I had no friends of my own, no family to talk to.

That was why I took up psychodrama, a kind of psychotherapy where the group members role-play parts in one another's personal dramas with the intention of mirroring buried feelings and insights. I had vague ideas of going on with the training and qualifying as a trainer. Perhaps that would give some meaning to my life beyond the shallow domestic life we led.

One Saturday, Michael did not go to golf.

His elder daughter, Natalie, and her boyfriend, had visited us a couple of weeks before and told us they were getting married. Natalie turned to me and said, 'Umm, I'm sorry, Anna, but we can't ask you because Mum will be there.'

Camilla and I had never been friends in England, though we moved in the same circle of friends. Now, she regarded me as the enemy who had stolen her man, even though he had left her months before he and I even thought of each other. She still regarded him as her husband, and would sometimes ring to speak to him. 'Hello? Is Michael there?' is all she would say to me.

The afternoon of the wedding, I went to a psychodrama workshop that lasted about three hours. After the workshop, I walked home through the park and my thoughts turned to Michael and the wedding and his family. Although his daughters were friendly to me, his parents would have nothing to do with me. He had told them that I'd left my daughters with my husband and he'd taken them to America. Or at least, that was their interpretation of what he said, and he didn't challenge it. He told me that his father would have been willing to meet me and welcome me into the family, but his mother was intransigent, and so he and his father humoured her. When he visited them and I was not included, I stayed home, walked in the park and raged to myself. I felt betrayed.

Michael told me his mother had been a constant wife and mother, living always for her family. She had never held a job and, apart from golf and tennis, had no friends or social life. She didn't drive, only went out with her husband, and never signed a cheque. I thought of my mother, who had worked in the Depression years when she had two little children, who ran the farm after my father left and, after he forced her to leave the farm, had returned to teaching. She kept working until she was in her late seventies.

I walked up the stairs to our first floor flat and let myself in. It was late afternoon. I had no idea when Michael would be home. Late, probably. I thought of him and Camilla pretending to be a family. I thought of my own family back in Sydney, and my daughters in Melbourne. I poured a glass of red wine from the cask and walked into the bedroom. I opened the wardrobe door and looked at his clothes. Lying in the shallow top drawer where he kept his ties and socks, I saw an elegant silk designer tie that Camilla had given him. It was midnight blue, a paisley pattern shot with rich gold and mustard and touches of emerald green. I got my sharp dressmaking scissors and shredded it in strips, then flushed them down the toilet. I left a remnant with the designer name on his pillow. With a refill of wine, I sat out on the balcony and brooded. Why had I followed him over here to live?

It must have been around that time that I had a dream that is still vivid in my mind over forty years later. I was in a forest clearing among a crowd of people. They started to move forward, and there was a feeling of panic and urgency. I resisted and stayed behind, watching them disappear over a rise. I moved forward to see where they had gone. Their bodies lay twisted and knotted together in a deep chasm. I turned and moved away. There was a spiral staircase beside me. A man was walking down it. At first, all I could see were his legs, bare, muscly, and his sandalled feet. His full body came into view. A well-set, stocky man with golden-olive skin, wearing an orange sarong. His head was shaven. He reached the foot of the stairs and I stepped forward. We embraced in an exquisite moment of union.

'Where have you been?' I asked.

'I've always been here, but you didn't see me.'

When I woke with a feeling of loss, I wondered what it meant. It seemed to me he was my guardian or my spirit guide who had been watching over me and who wanted me to know I was not alone and I need not fear annihilation. I was lost, but my life had meaning I could not yet see. He came to remind me of that.

Apart from a sense of my pathway in life, whatever that might be, which had been confirmed for me by the visitor on the spiral staircase, my love for my children kept me going. The union with Michael was disappointing. The poetry and passion of his letters dissolved in daily life.

Some time after I shredded the tie, perhaps on another occasion when I was excluded from one of his family gatherings, I took all the letters he'd written me during our year of courtship and burnt them in a bin in the park.

'You're different from how you were when we wrote to each other,' I told him.

'It's not the same,' he said.

We were both disappointed, then. He was doing what he'd always done, holding on to routine, family, work and golf. He was living in the city he'd grown up in and wasn't willing to take risks, unless you count the one he'd taken in asking me to join in his life. He wanted me to be the piece that filled the empty space in his jigsaw and I wasn't quite the right shape.

It was I who had taken the bigger risk, leaving everything and everyone I knew and loved to come to a strange city where his family excluded me, and my daughters were on the other side of the desert. No wonder he couldn't fill the space in my heart. He was a second chance after all my failures to find an equal, intimate love, and he seemed like second best.

I thought back to the last time I'd dreamed of finding a real connection with a man. I'd given my heart to my lawyer. He was my lifeline after I lost my children, and he loved me as I was but always kept me separate from the rest of his life. When I was in despair after leaving my little girls behind, I told him my story. He listened and said little.

After several cups of coffee and a couple of cigarettes, he said, 'Anna, you don't have a problem. What has happened is not your fault. You did the best you could in impossible circumstances. All is not lost. Things change when you least expect them to.'

His words resonated in my head and kept me alive in those dreadful days.

We became lovers, but it was always on his terms. I was his bolthole from a pressured professional life and an unhappy marriage. He was my lifeline. Finally, I cut the cord but it wasn't a clean cut. For years after I stopped being his lover because it was too painful, I longed for him, and whenever I saw him, it was like the first time. I believed then that I would never love a man as I loved him. If he is still alive, he would be ninety-three. I often wonder about him, and still, occasionally, I dream about him. But the dreams are always the same…there are other people around, we can't be together, or if we are, it is brief and interrupted. He is called away or he disappears.

I held on to the desire to have a second family. I knew my daughters could never be with me while they were children, and I longed for a child who could grow up with me, whom I could love and nurture and keep safe. Michael had agreed to try for a child of our own, but when I spoke of it, he expressed his fears. He had lost two little boys in their infancy. The first was a cot death. When the second child was a toddler, he fell ill with a fever. They'd been invited to a party. Camilla had arranged a babysitter and insisted on going.

'What happened?'

'We got home late, after midnight. Camilla checked on him and said he was OK, not to disturb him, he was asleep. We went to bed and made love. Then I got up and went in to check on him. He was feverish and pale and his pulse was racing. I called the doctor and they took him to hospital. But it was too late. They couldn't save him. He died the next day.'

Michael hated talking about it, but sometimes when he'd had a couple of glasses of wine, he shared disturbing thoughts…that Camilla had neglected her babies, perhaps even wanted them to die.

'She had a strange childhood. Her mother was mentally ill, diagnosed as schizophrenic, and was put in an institution when Camilla was three years old. It was a big Catholic family, six kids. Her sisters brought her up. Once, my parents went round to visit her when the second boy was a baby. She wasn't there. They could hear him crying, but they couldn't get in. They waited and she turned up. She'd been out to the shops to get something, she said. That wasn't the only incident.'

I wondered why he had stayed with her all those years. There were other things that happened that strained their marriage. It seemed he had pushed them aside and kept on, trying to be a good father and husband and provider, until it all got too much for him and he had to walk away.

So there we were, two damaged people trying to make a life together and have our own family. We both wanted a family, a loving, safe circle. His own family had been claustrophobic, inward-looking and conservative, with a matriarch who had never been an independent woman and had no life outside the domestic circle. His marriage became a trap in which he had been the provider and stabiliser. His wife had kept up the charade of sacred marriage (she was a devout Roman Catholic) while she lived her private hell and subjected him and her children to it.

He sought a woman who would meet his desires and give him a family space he could feel safe in.

When I was young, I sought a man who would fill the hole my father had left, but I had fallen into the net of patriarchy. When I broke out of it, I lost my babies. In my fortieth year, I sought a man who would see me and hold me without trying to shape me to his formula. I chose a man who was still bound by his birth family and his Medusa marriage.

Six

I'm at the gynaecologist's rooms. I've been with Michael six months now and haven't yet got pregnant.

'Are there any issues with your sex life?' he asks, pushing his rimless glasses back up his nose.

'Well…yes. It's painful for me. He's…big, and I'm small, and it hurts quite a lot sometimes.'

'What are your periods like? Are they regular? Is the flow light, or heavy? You're in your fortieth year, and it may be you're starting early menopause.'

'They're regular, but I have strong cramps and a heavy flow for the first three days.'

'Do you have pain in between?'

'Yes, especially when I have a bowel motion.'

'Hmm. I'll need to do an internal examination.'

After examining me, he peels off his gloves and sits at his desk. I get dressed and sit down in front of him.

He takes his glasses off, thinks for a moment, then says, 'I think you have endometriosis. What happens is that the specialised cells that make up the lining of your uterus grow outside and attach to the walls of the vagina and other parts.'

'What's the treatment?'

He puts his glasses on again and looks at me. 'Well, getting pregnant would be the cure. But the catch-22 is, it's difficult if not impossible to get pregnant when you have endometriosis. Hormone treatment is possible, but I don't recommend it because of the side effects. Surgery can remove the excess tissue, but it will regrow. Removal of the uterus and the ovaries would be the last resort. Really, Anna, I'm sorry to say, your chances of getting pregnant are very slight. But I should do a laparoscopy to confirm the diagnosis.'

'What is that?'

'We give a local anaesthetic and put a tube in through the belly button so we can see what's going on inside.'

I walk out of his office feeling sad. I've come so far, lost so much, and this is my last chance for a family. Time is running out. I'm not giving up. I step into the lift and press the button.

The laparoscopy confirms his diagnosis.

On Sundays, Michael and I go to the Satyananda ashram for satsang. I am surprised to find that he is open to ways of being and knowing beyond the scientific limits of his education. His father is Jewish but not religious, and he is an atheist. He is strongly rational and sceptical of Eastern philosophies and mystical beliefs. Yet he finds relaxation after the tension of holding the bodily positions of the asanas, and resonates to the energy of the satsang, the sense of community, the chanting, the simple vegetable curries and rice, the friendliness and acceptance. The two swamis, Krishnamurti, the elder, who is tall and thin and ascetic, and Tapasmurti, the junior, who is short and chubby and cheerful, treat us like family. For me, it is all the family I have here apart from Michael.

'Krishna,' I say when I can take him aside for a quiet moment, 'I'd like to ask your advice.'

He beckons me into a quiet room and we sit cross-legged on the mat. There is a faint smell of sandalwood incense, and I can hear the chatter and laughter in the other room.

'Michael and I want to have a child. You know I lost my three daughters.'

He nods.

'Well, I've tried to get pregnant with no luck, and now, my doctor tells me I won't be able to because I have endometriosis.'

I explain what that means, and he listens, then picks up the book that is their bible, *Asana Pranayama Mudra Bandha*. He thumbs through it, then turns to the index and puts a cross beside several entries. Then he hands it to me. 'Do these asanas every morning at dawn for the next six months. You will be surprised.'

'Oh, thank you. How much do I owe you?'

'It is our gift. Go well.' He smiles a rare, warm smile and hugs me. His body is taut and firm, his arms strong, and I feel his steadiness and serenity seeping into my heart.

I've never got up at dawn before unless I've had to, like for an early shift at work, but I do what Krishna has said, and Michael gets up with me and does some poses and breathing.

Our life trudges on. I'm now working as outpatients sister in the psychiatric unit at Royal Perth Hospital. The job is routine, mostly seeing long-term outpatients suffering from schizophrenia or some other chronic condition. I check on how they are going before the doctor sees them and give them an injection if they're due for it. I try to extend my role by taking on low-key counselling with some patients who need someone to talk to about what's going on in their lives.

Michael decides we should stop renting and buy a house; two-bedroom units are soulless and cramped when my daughters visit, and if we do have a child, we'll need more room. He doesn't have much money for a deposit, so we search for an older house that is affordable.

Mount Lawley is an older suburb on the fringes of inner Perth, bordered by Hyde Park and the Swan River. The train line runs through it. It's one of those areas where many of the settler descendants live; it has a faded respectability overlaid with trendy new cafés and a sprinkling of students and artists. We find a house near the train line, with lots of character and a good, deep piece of land. It's unrenovated but affordable. It has an inner quiet and peace I like, and a feeling of age and continuity. A refuge in this shallow city. Maybe this will be our forever house.

A long weekend comes up, and we plan to go camping. It will be the first time we've spent more than one day together since I came over here. Car packed with camping gear and food, we head towards Cervantes, a fishing port two hours north of Perth. We plan to camp wherever we can off road, not in a formal campsite.

Our spot is a bit inland among sandy dunes with a scattering of she-oak trees. Once we've set the tent up, I find kindling and start a fire. I love cooking over a wood fire, the smoke in my eyes, the smell of burning sticks, the sap sizzling in the green ends. It takes me back to childhood and the open fireplaces in our long living room. But even better, because the night air enfolds us, the wind rustles through the she-oak needles, and after dark, a mournful two-note call sounds in a distant tree.

'A powerful owl,' Michael says. 'They nest in hollows in large eucalypts.'

We sit by the glowing coals after our simple meal and sip cask wine.

'Where shall we camp tomorrow? I'd like to see Kalbarri and the gorges.'

'Ah,' says Michael, staring into the fire, 'I don't think we'll get that far.'

'Why not?'

'I'm playing in a match on Monday morning with a mate. We'll have to head back on Sunday.'

'What? This is our first time away together since I came over here, and you arranged this without talking to me about it?'

'Well, I'm not playing on Saturday, so I thought we'd have two days together…'

'How could you? Fucking golf! It's all you think about at the weekends. I might as well not be here.' I rage on and drink more wine, letting out all the anger I've shut up tight inside me since I came over here.

Michael gets up and starts cleaning the dishes and putting things away. He walks off and leaves me to it. By the time he comes back, I'm on my fourth glass. My shouting shifts to crying. He does his best to ignore me and goes to bed.

Another glass. I wish I'd never come over here. I wish I could go home. There's nothing to keep me here. My job is boring, I've got no friends, Michael loves his golf more than me, his family don't want to know me…

Spent, I throw sand on the last of the fire and go into the tent. I pull off my clothes and drop down onto the mattress beside Michael. He turns to me and takes me in his arms, and we make love. His shouts and my moans ring out through the night. We might be the last couple on the planet, dying as we make love for the last time.

A few weeks later, I return to Dr Smith to tell him my period is three weeks overdue.

He does an examination and looks at me with a small smile as he pulls off his gloves. 'Well, I'm glad to say you are pregnant. And I must say I'm very surprised.'

I don't tell him about my dawn rituals or our wild love scene.

My life will get better now I have started on the journey of motherhood again.

One night, over dinner, Michael clears his throat and blinks. This is always a sign he has something on his mind.

'What is it, Michael?'

'When is the girls' next visit?'

'I told you, they'll be with us for Christmas. After our baby is born.' He's due early in December.

'How much leave will you take from work?'

'Oh, I'm not sure. I'd like to take at least six months… I don't want to put him in day care before I have to.'

'Well, you know, if you're not working, we won't be able to afford for the girls to come over.'

'But…I can't do that. I only see them twice a year as it is. You can't ask me not to see them at all.'

He stands up and walks over to the sink, starts scraping dishes and washing up. 'I don't earn much, Anna. I can't afford to pay for their fares on top of our mortgage and living expenses.'

'But Michael, I can't not see them. I'll borrow money. I'll do anything I have to to see them.'

He thumps a glass down on the draining board and it shatters. He turns to face me and yells, 'We can't do the impossible. If we don't have the money from your income, we can't afford for them to come.' He walks off down the hall, out the front door, slamming it behind him.

This argument continues for days, with the air stretched tight and thin between us. I feel miserable and trapped. Again, I wonder why I followed him over here.

On Saturday morning before he leaves for golf, I say, 'Michael, if we can't afford for the girls to visit us here, I'll leave you. I'll go and live in Melbourne near the girls and I'll have the baby there.'

When he comes home, we don't speak. He sleeps in the spare bedroom and we spend Sunday in silence.

This goes on for a few days, and I start to make plans for leaving. I get a Melbourne paper and look for jobs in psychiatric units, and for places to rent in suburbs near where the girls live. I'm horrified at the rentals and begin to wonder if I should just go back to Sydney and stay with Mum for a while until I find a job and somewhere to live.

Michael comes home from work at the end of the week and asks me to sit out in the garden with him. He opens a bottle of white wine… we usually drink cask, but since I've known I am pregnant, I only have a glass or two.

Under the jacaranda tree, we sit on two old cane chairs on the brick paving he's been laying.

'I'm taking a job in the Pilbara, as manager of the pharmacy at Wickham. It's fairly well paid, so we'll be able to pay the girls' fares at Christmas time, and you won't have to go back to work while the baby is little.'

I'm lost for words. He's so secretive. He hasn't told me anything about this until it's a fait accompli. But I can see it's a solution.

I don't really care where we live, as long as I have my baby and I can see my girls.

Seven

Wickham is a town of a thousand or so people in the north-west of WA. The sun beats down on the tin roof of the little house. There are no trees or shrubs around, just bare flat ragged grass, and beyond, more of the same box-shaped houses. All air-conditioned twenty-four hours a day.

In the monotony of this boxed life, I am happy. I hang the washing out at seven a.m., before the sun gets too high, and walk down to the shops after breakfast. Even so, wearing a hat and suncream, I get burnt. Fresh fruit and vegetables are expensive, and the choice is limited. Meat is pricey too.

Michael tells me that his boss rings him once a week to see how many watches and cameras he's sold. 'He wants me to sell people prescription drugs, like tranquillisers, that they don't have scripts for. Apparently, the last manager did and so they expect it.'

'Do you?'

'No, of course not. I've told him I can't do that.'

He is tense and shut off, which is how he gets when he has things on his mind. In bed, he groans in his sleep, grinds his teeth and tosses and turns. I'm in my second trimester and nothing worries me. The baby is due mid-December, and the girls are booked to fly to Perth a few days before Christmas. Then they'll fly to Karratha, the nearest airport.

I've been to see the GP here and told him that my gynaecologist says I should return to Perth two weeks before the baby's due.

'He says I need to have specialist care because it's eleven years since I've had a baby and I'm forty, so I'm high risk.'

'Does he? Well, all seems normal to me. The baby is growing well, your blood pressure's normal, you're healthy, I see no reason why you can't have an easy birth like you had with your daughters.'

'That's good. But…what if something does go wrong?'

'We've got the flying doctor. We can fly you up to Port Hedland. There are specialist obstetricians there. But I deliver babies here all the time.'

It's November. I thought it couldn't get any hotter, but it does. I've given up walking to the shops and give Michael a shopping list so he can get one of the assistants to go to the supermarket.

Our only respite is on Sundays when the pharmacy is shut and we drive to Point Samson, a little fishing port a few miles west. The beach is safe, within a semicircle of craggy red-brown rocks, and we swim in the shallow water. Or rather, Michael does his lazy crawl, stretching his long, thin body out in the turquoise folds of the water, and I paddle, getting wet up to my neck, cooling off, letting the baby in my belly be rocked by the gentle wavelets. Nothing matters here; all is gentle and easy. I know no harm can come to him or to me; the birth will be easy, Michael will find his feet in the pharmacy and become respected, and we can stay here while our baby is young and needs my care. My daughters will visit us and we will bring them here at weekends and have fish and chips on the beach at sunset.

Michael comes home early one Friday and throws his keys on the kitchen table. 'We have to go back to Perth.'

'Shit, why? What's happened?'

'I've been sacked.'

Slowly, I extract the story. His voice is low and flat and his eyes don't meet mine. His boss says he hasn't met expectations.

'What does that mean?'

'You tell me! I suppose I haven't sold enough fucking watches and cameras or dispensed enough drugs without a script. Two weeks' notice.'

Strangely, I'm not worried. Maybe it's the baby hormones. Michael is more withdrawn than usual. I don't think about what we'll do back in Perth, where we'll live, how we'll support ourselves. We have just $2,000 in the bank. But the girls' fares are paid, and Michael, to my surprise, does not suggest cancelling them.

All our stuff is packed, the little bits of furniture we brought and the crockery I've bought here (the house was only partly furnished). I've carefully labelled things: 'Pack', 'Leave here'. The day we catch the plane to Perth, at ten thirty a.m. on 30 November, the temperature is forty-five degrees. When we arrive in Perth, it's twenty-three degrees.

I visit Dr Smith for a check-up.

He sits, as always, for a minute or two after he's examined me, looking down at his notepad. Then he looks at me over his glasses and says, 'Well, Anna, all seems well. But I think we may have our dates wrong. I think you should come into hospital early next week and I'll induce the baby. I think he's almost ready.'

We've been staying with Michael's married daughter, and I've used the days searching for a flat. I find a little terrace house on the edge of Mount Lawley, where we had that forever house for a few months before our Pilbara adventure. The rent is affordable, forty dollars a week. We move in at the weekend, making do with some borrowed furniture while we wait for our stuff to arrive from Wickham. It's a Federation-style brick terrace, with a tiny strip of garden in front, two bedrooms, a living room, kitchen and bathroom and a little back garden that is mostly sand with a few stray vincas and an olive tree. It's close to the main street, so I can walk to the shops with the baby in the pram.

Meanwhile, Michael has set up to do locum work, which means he does relief work anywhere around the city for a week or more at a time when pharmacists go on leave. There's no security, but it's better paid than a regular salary when the work is there.

I'm lying in bed in a private room in hospital, with a drip in my arm.

The contractions are slow and heavy, crunching down my spine, and I can't ride them.

They engulf me and take me into a cave where there are looming dark shapes and the air is heavy and foetid and I can't get my breath.

Aaaarggh! My baby will be born deformed; his spine is pressing on mine; he is hunchback like his grandfather. This is what his father fears, a curse that has been put on him by his first wife who seeks revenge on me for taking her husband. She wants our baby to die like her first two boy babies. She is an evil witch who has cast a spell over him. He escaped into my love, but he is still under her spell and the spell of his birth, his passive-aggressive mother, his repressed father, his parochial upbringing.

Why did I come to this place and join my life with his?

Ah, I remember. I wanted to have a child and he wanted me. I can't go back.

Dr Smith walks in and checks my chart. He asks the nurse how close the contractions are, then steps up to me and palpates my belly.

'I can't keep doing this!'

'Come on, Anna, you can do this.'

'I fucking can't!'

He steps away and speaks to the nurse, then comes close again. 'OK, I'll give you a caudal anaesthetic. You may still feel pressure, but you won't feel the pain of the contractions. But it means that when the time comes, because your hips and legs are effectively paralysed, you won't be able to push to help the baby come out. So we may need to give him some help, perhaps with forceps.'

The afternoon drags on, and the nurse who is specialling me checks the screen on the monitor at my bedside. The leads are attached to a cap on the baby's head to monitor his vital signs.

Michael comes in after work and sits beside me.

'How are the girls?' I say, shifting my shoulders on the firm mattress. It feels weird not to be able to move my legs. 'Are they OK?' They arrived yesterday after I was admitted for the induction, so I haven't seen them yet. This time, it's just Caitlin and Penelope. Sophia is away on a school camp and will be here next week, just before Christmas.

'They're fine. Excited to be here. I left Caitlin in charge, and they've got pizza for tea.'

Caitlin is thirteen, Penelope ten going on eleven.

The nurse walks in at about seven thirty and does an internal examination. 'Ah, I think the baby's ready to come! I'll call the doctor.'

Ten minutes later, Dr Smith walks in the door. He takes one look at the monitor screen and says, 'That baby's distressed!' He mutters something to the nurse and pulls the end of the table out, nearly breaking her foot. Ignoring her repressed cry, he tells her to call for support.

Seconds later, two nurses and a doctor hurry in.

I am spreadeagled, knees up and apart, and a nurse is swabbing me while the doctor grabs an instrument like a pair of elongated salad tongs and steps up to the table, putting one hand on my belly while he inserts the tongs. Seconds pass. I feel a pulling, a dragging, and then a vacuum. I can't see what is happening below me; no one speaks. Dr Smith passes a bundled shape to the other doctor, who steps quickly across to a side table.

Michael is gripping my hand and we are both holding our breath, waiting for the baby's cry. I don't know what Michael is thinking, but I imagine he's remembering his two little boys who died. Ah, please let this baby live. Please let him be healthy and normal.

Seconds pass that seem like hours. At last, a raucous cry, like a baby galah calling for food, rings out, and Michael hugs me. His tears meet mine.

The baby is checked and sponged and wrapped in a clean, soft cloth before they let me hold him.

Eighth of December 1980. The beginning of the second half of my life.

Dr Smith steps over and grasps my hand. 'Well, Anna, I'm happy to say you and Michael have a healthy baby boy. We just got him out in time. The cord was wrapped around his neck and he'd inhaled meconium, so we had to suck his tubes out so he could breathe. The reason the labour was so painful was that it was a dry labour, and his spine was against yours.'

Michael and I gently unwrap him and check his chest and his spine. He doesn't have Michael's pigeon chest or his grandfather's deformed spine. He seems a perfectly healthy little baby, long-limbed, with a reddish glow to his skin, no jaundice. He has golden hair and brown eyes like his father. His hair will probably turn dark like Michael's. I'm glad. I wanted a brown-eyed boy.

Later, when he lies in my arms and Michael has gone home to tell the girls they have a baby brother, the nurse comes in and strokes his soft head and says, 'It was a close shave. His apgars were one when he was born. Five minutes later, they were nine.'

Apgars are a measurement of vital signs – appearance, pulse, reflexes, skin colour, muscle tone – when a baby is born. Each is rated out of two, adding up to ten. So, one out of ten…all but dead. Nine out of ten – normal and healthy.

If Michael hadn't been sacked, if we hadn't come back to Perth, if my baby had been born in the Pilbara, he would have died. If I hadn't had an induction, if the nurse hadn't called the doctor, if he hadn't come in time, if he hadn't done a forceps delivery, he would have died. I was so sure I could have a normal delivery up there. But the dates were wrong; we would have waited too long.

Eight

When the baby, whom we've named Sebastian after Michael's father, is about twenty months old, I take him with me to visit Mum. She had come over to visit us when he was new and stayed for a week. It was an ordeal for her. She had to be taken on and off the plane in a wheelchair. She quietly took her place in our little terrace house, and I took her on some outings and a shopping expedition to the dress shop in the main street, where she bought a couple of new outfits.

One day, walking through the living room to her bedroom, she tripped on a rug and fell. I was nursing the baby. Michael rushed over to her and helped her up, but she brushed him off and went to her room. When she emerged, her eyes were red. She is so proud, she hates to admit she is losing her independence. She hates being helped.

I talked to her then about coming to live with us. Michael agreed, though he's never liked her. She is reserved and he finds her patronising. I think they are jealous of each other. In the end, she simply didn't reply to my invitation. Although she misses me, it is too late in her life for her to make that transition. She is comfortable and secure and relatively independent in her granny flat, and David and Jo are in the background. With us, she wouldn't have her own space. And perhaps she knows that this marriage is built on shaky ground.

I am not Mum's favourite child. David, her firstborn, has always been her golden boy. But when she and I lived together through those years after Dad left and I helped her as best I could with running the farm and looking after the animals, she came to rely on me.

My Sydney visit is disappointing. I want her to know Sebastian before she dies, but she seems withdrawn. More involved in the papers, her books and the TV shows she always watches, and less interested in me and Sebastian. I feel that she has given up, somehow, since I went to live in Perth. In Sydney, I was a centre point in her life…my weekly visits for dinner, my phone calls, the films we saw together or the occasional lunches in town. She lived for the holidays when my girls would visit. Now, she hardly sees them, except once when Robert arranged for them to stay overnight with her when they were travelling back from a visit to his family in Mackay.

On this visit, I become more aware of how tired I am. Sebastian still wakes at night to breastfeed. When he was new, I was feeding him every two hours. He seemed to be hungry all the time. The clinic sister told me to supplement his feeds with a bottle. He got the nickname Pod, because he was chubby and loved his bottle. I am his night-time comfort.

One afternoon, I visit friends with him. Rachel is a psychiatrist, Richard is a paediatric physician. I tell them of my broken nights, and they shake their heads.

'You're making a rod for your own back,' Richard says. 'He doesn't need the extra nourishment now, he wants the comfort of suckling. You need to do controlled crying.'

'How do you do that?'

'Sleep in another room. When he cries, go in and pick him up and reassure him, then put him down again. He'll probably start crying again. They forget why they're crying. Let him cry for a few minutes. Then go in and pick him up again, soothe him and lay him down again. He'll probably cry for less time, and then he'll go back to sleep.'

'How many nights will I need to do that for?'

'Maybe a couple. He'll soon learn to sleep through.'

It works, but I feel terrible and make sure I give him more attention, more cuddles, more play time during the day. My beautiful boy I waited so long for, so many dark years, such a difficult birth, so nearly lost. He is my new life, the life I longed for.

I thought I would find it with a man. I was wrong. It was a child I needed. He does not replace my lost girls, but he gives me the hope and belief in motherhood and childhood that I lost that day I left them, when Robert forced me to return to Sydney, threatening to kill me, kill them and kill himself if I tried to take them from him.

I don't want to burden Sebastian with this past horror. I want him to be free and happy and grow up in the shape he chooses, not one chosen for him by me or by his father. To become who he is meant to be… himself. My long-limbed, brown-eyed boy.

Nine

One day at work, I get a phone call from David.

'Why are you calling me at work? What's wrong?'

'I'm sorry, sis. Mum died early this morning, about three a.m.'

I knew she was in hospital but I didn't realise it was the end of her life.

'Did you know she was dying?'

'Well, it's complicated. It's nearly three months she's been in hospital, and they were about to transfer her to a nursing home because they need the bed. Vera went to see her last night, and she seemed all right then.'

'Why didn't you tell me how ill she was?'

'Honestly, sis, we didn't realise.'

I put the phone down and sit in my office chair. My chest and throat burn and I feel a tight band around my heart.

The story Vera, my sister, tells me when I go over for the funeral is that when she visited Mum that last night, Mum said, 'I'm so afraid that this is the end.'

'What did you say?'

'I tried to reassure her. I said, "Of course it's not. You'll pull through, like you always do. Please don't die. We don't want you to die!" I said goodnight and went home.'

'Did the hospital call you to let you know she was dying?'

'Apparently they did, but I had earplugs in so I could sleep.'

I choke back an angry response. I would have listened to her, asked her about her fears, tried to share with her those threshold moments. And I wouldn't have put earplugs in! I would have sat with her.

I've never been with a dying person. My father died at ninety-seven and a half in a nursing home in a Queensland town. I visited him twice in his last years: once when he was ninety-five and still living with his son and son's partner, and again when we both knew it would be the last time. We said goodbye then. He'd abandoned his family when I was a young child, had made no effort to keep in touch with me. He came back when I was fourteen and away at boarding school and turned my mother off the farm so he could sell it. After all those years she'd kept it going with help from me and my brothers when they were home from school or university.

My mother was my loyal and steadfast parent who stood by me in those terrible years after I lost my children. She even went with me to Colorado on my first access visit, braving the winter and a strange city in a country she considered corrupt and decadent, staying in the home of my daughters' abductor.

I don't believe that no one in the Sydney family realised she was dying. If they didn't, it must have been wilful blindness.

David takes me to see her in her coffin the day before the funeral. Her skin is grey and stretched tight over her gaunt, bony face. Her nose is beaky, more prominent than when she was alive. Such sadness, such loss in those features.

Yet her life was in many ways a triumph. She brought us five children up, saw that we had a good education, that we were able to do things we had gifts for, and was a loving and devoted grandmother. She had been a staunch partner to Dad all those years of drought, the Great Depression, dust storms and loss of stock. Just as the seasons were starting to improve, he decided he'd had enough and walked off. He promised to sign the farm over to her if she brought us up and educated us. But he didn't keep his promise. He turned her away with nothing but a suitcase. She had to fight in the courts to get a share of the sale; she was allotted one-third of the sale price, eight thousand pounds.

She went back to teaching; threw her heart and soul into it. She finally retired in her late seventies and tried to find ways of filling in her

time. She had learned to drive in her fifties when Dad left, taught by my brothers. She wasn't a good driver, but on our quiet dirt roads not much harm could happen, apart from the truck breaking down out in the paddocks, or getting bogged in the deep, muddy ruts at the side of the road after rain.

Wisely, she didn't drive when she lived in the city. While she was teaching, she would get a lift into the city with David or get the ferry and buses to work. After she retired, she helped in a meals centre for homeless people for a while, serving, clearing tables and washing up. Eventually, she had to give that up too. Then her days were regulated by the early morning cup of tea, reading the paper or her latest book about the ancient Greek and Roman world or the Middle East, preparing and eating simple meals, and watching the ABC at night.

Once, when I visited her, she said, 'You know, I wonder sometimes why I'm still alive.'

'What do you mean, Mum?'

'All my life, I've found meaning by serving others. Now I can't do that, I feel my life has no purpose.'

How sad, I thought. To feel that life is empty when one can't work. I promise myself I will not live for others. I will live for myself, and service to others will come out of that core of being. One of my favourite poets, Gerard Manly Hopkins, says it for me:

> Each mortal thing does one thing and the same:
> Selves – goes itself; myself it speaks and spells;
> Crying What I do is me: for that I came.

Ten

It's Saturday morning, six months since Mum died. I'm sitting in a salon. My hairdresser is tying my hair up in tight curlers for an afro perm. The assistant helping her is talking about her training as a clairvoyant.

How can you train to be a clairvoyant, I wonder. Surely you either are or you aren't.

The assistant looks at me and says, 'There's a woman around you. Has someone you're close to died recently?'

'Yes,' I say and burst into tears. 'My mother,' I manage between sobs. It is the first time I've cried since Mum's funeral, which I sat through with tears flooding down my face while the minister ranted on about the resurrection.

'There, there,' the hairdresser said, patting my shoulder and shaking her head at the assistant.

'It's OK,' I say, wiping my eyes and blowing my nose. 'It's just that I wasn't there when she died. I hadn't seen her for several months. I didn't know she was dying.'

The assistant handed the hairdresser another curler and put her hand on my shoulder. 'You know, our loved ones stay around the earthly plane for a while when they pass. When we think about them and mourn them, it draws them back and holds them near us. Eventually, we need to let go of them so they can move on.'

The hairdresser shrugs and pats a strip of cotton wool in place under the curlers, across my forehead and under my ears. 'Go and get me a cap for her head, please,' she says to the assistant, as she dabs the perm solution onto the tight rows.

About an hour later, I'm sitting under the dryer.

The assistant comes over to me to check if my hair is dry. She turns the dryer off and pushes it away from my head. 'I'm sorry I upset you,' she says as she starts to unroll the curlers.

'Oh, not at all. I'm glad you said what you did.'

'There's something else she wants you to know.'

'What is it?'

'She said not to feel guilty, that all is forgiven.'

Bloody Mum! I suppose I'm to be forgiven for leaving my children, for leaving her and coming to Perth, for not being there when she died. I'm in the wrong again.

In retrospect, I think what she meant was that she understood, not just why I left her and went to Perth, and why I couldn't be there when she died, but everything that happened. That she no longer felt betrayed and deserted and that she saw why I needed to do the things she found so hard to accept at the time. That she could see the cycles of abandonment and loss in her life and mine and my children's, and that she is present still at some level I cannot perceive or grasp, loving us, helping us to get through, to learn and take something joyful and loving from what happens to us.

Eleven

Sebastian will be four at the end of this year, 1984. He goes to home day care. He hates it. Each morning when I take him there, I have to drag him out of the car, hand him to the day care mother, Daphne, whom he calls Duckling, leave him crying, and drive to work. I'm running the psych unit, inpatients, day hospital, outpatients and community care while the charge nurse is in England on study leave, so at least I don't have to do much shift work, just a weekend once a month to give the other nurses a break.

Michael is still doing locum work, and we've graduated from the little terrace house in North Perth to a small house on an estate in Perth's northern suburbs. It seemed ideal because the estate is small, each house with its private garden, and a shared garden space in the centre with little groves of native shrubs and rocks, a few garden seats scattered around. We should be happy in this pleasant house surrounded by bushland, with the little boy we both dreamed of.

But we're not.

We have drifted farther apart than before. Michael is lovely with Sebastian, cuddling him and playing with him when he's home, putting him to sleep at night with tunes on his penny whistle, and telling him funny animal stories he's made up. With me, he is remote and withdrawn a lot of the time. He works like an automaton and doesn't talk about it at home, probably because it's so boring.

My work, by contrast, is volatile and stressful; not so much because of the patients, whom I've never found difficult, but because of the staff. I wasn't a popular appointment as relief charge, as I'd been working in outpatients, and the inpatient staff resent me. Their favourite, an officious, overly friendly little man called Mike, is my second-in-charge. He works insidiously to undermine me. I try to put some reforms in place, like having a community meeting with the patients each week on the lines of a therapeutic community. The staff go through the motions with it but clearly think it is a waste of time, which it is, mostly, since we get new patients and discharge others all the time, so there is no continuity.

I have to deal with rotten apples in the basket, one after another. Mike's best friend Alastair, the other staff favourite, is having an affair with one of the student nurses seconded to our unit. He turns up to shifts late, often hungover, and talks to everyone about his conflicts with his wife and their separation. One of the junior nurses misses some of her shifts without notice, and when I try to find out what her problem is, I discover she is on drugs. We are often short-staffed. One shift, I have to assign a student nurse to do close obs on a psychotic patient who is diagnosed with obsessive compulsive disorder and is having a trial of a new drug to try and settle her. If anything, it has depressed her and she is fairly inactive, so it seems safe enough to put a student nurse with her. But it is an open ward with no locked doors and people coming and going all the time. It's difficult to keep track of someone if they don't follow routine.

At morning tea, the patient cannot be found. I send a couple of staff out to search the grounds, but there is no sight of her. We notify admin and they say they will call the police.

Half an hour later, a policeman comes and asks to see me. 'Do you have a patient called Rose Mortimer?' he says, twiddling his cap in his hands.

'Yes, but she's been missing for about an hour.'

'We found her body at the trainline. She put her head on the line when a train was approaching.'

The shock of this brings us together, trying to support each other and deal with the red tape, while admin take care of notifying the family. We are coping, but Rose's psychiatrist calls a meeting, supposedly to support us. He spends the hour cross-examining us, especially me, and implies it is our fault. I sit in shock, trying to answer his questions and hold myself together. When he leaves the meeting, I rush into the charge nurse's cubicle, followed by Mike and Alastair. I burst into tears and we hug each other.

A rare moment of solidarity under attack. The next worst thing is when I discover that one of the day hospital patients has taken an overdose. She survives, but it comes out that she's been intimate with the day hospital sister. I interview the sister and realise she is schizophrenic. I get the psychiatrist in charge of day hospital to assess her. He agrees with me. I tell admin and they refuse to do anything about it. I think they are afraid of union action. I have to talk to her every day until, at last, I persuade her to take sick leave. She doesn't return.

All this stress has taken its toll on me, and now we have a new challenge in our little family.

The Family Law Act has changed to allow children to choose which parent they will live with without having to go to court once they turn fourteen. Penelope has told me she wants to come and live with us, and we get the third bedroom ready for her. I am overjoyed, yet afraid. The balance of my marriage is so delicate. I wonder how Michael will react to having my daughter with us, whether he will be able to make her welcome and part of the family.

Robert phones me to tell me that her passport needs to be renewed and he wants me to sign the form. He wants to take her on an overseas trip before she comes over here. I refuse to sign until he signs an agreement that he will not try and stop her from coming to live with me. Maybe he plans to keep her with him. The older two girls have left home, so she is all he has left. We argue back and forth for a while, and Penelope phones me in tears and pleads with me to sign. He must be putting pressure on her.

Come she does after the school year has started. It feels unreal, to have my fourteen-year-old daughter living with us. The first time she's lived with me for more than a holiday since she was just over two years old. It takes time to adjust to it, to create a routine of family life that is stable and loving for her, between school, my work and Michael's, day care and home. The best part is to see her bonding with her little brother, who quickly becomes very attached to her. She cuddles him, plays with him, sings to him, bathes him and tells him stories at bedtime. They both have what they have missed. She, a little brother to love as she wanted to be loved when she was little. He, a big sister to be his playmate and third parent.

Michael is jealous, though he tries not to show it. He is kind to Penelope most of the time, but then, for no reason, he will grumble and pick on her for trivial things. He's much the same with me, but when he's in a bad mood, he ramps it up. He's done so since the first few months we were together. I never know when it will happen.

When Sebastian was a baby, I took on the role of nurse in charge on night duty at weekends, three nights, so I could be with him during the day. I tried to sleep for a few hours during the day while Michael looked after Sebastian. I took an antidepressant tablet Michael recommended to help me to sleep, and a glass or two of stout to switch off my thoughts. I'd go into a doze for a while, but I couldn't sleep. In our small two-bedroom flat, I could hear the baby crying. Michael would take him out to the golf course later in the morning and hit a few practice balls with Sebastian in the stroller.

One Monday, I was feeling ragged. After three nights on duty and not much sleep, I felt tense and low. I could see no end to this way of life. I had asked admin to put me back on day shifts. I would find day care for Sebastian and try to balance mothering him with work. But they refused, saying I must carry on with night duty until they could find a replacement.

Sebastian was asleep at last, and I was throwing together an evening meal and sipping red wine when Michael came home from work. He was quite cheerful, probably because he was off baby duties, which he didn't enjoy.

We made conversation over dinner, and when I stood up to clear the plates, he said, 'Jenny's having an engagement party this weekend.'

'Oh, great.' I liked Jenny, Michael's niece, and the guy she planned to marry.

'Where is she having it?'

'At her dad's house. But…Camilla will be there.'

'Ah, so I can't go.'

'That's right.'

I slammed the plates down. 'I'm sick of this! I'm sick of being treated like the other woman! I had nothing to do with your marriage break-up. Your family treat me as a stranger, like I don't belong. Your parents only agreed to meet me when Sebastian was about to be born. When your daughter got married, you played happy families with Camilla and I had to stay away. Now your niece is getting married and it's the same thing. I thought your brother and I got on well when I first met him. But like you, he's too weak to stand up to Camilla and tell her that I'm your wife and I will be at family celebrations. Then she could choose whether she wants to be there or not. It's time you acted like my husband and told him to shape up.'

Michael glared at me and walked out. When he came back an hour later, I was still angry. I'd picked Sebastian up and fed and settled him again and was washing up the dishes. He stalked into the kitchen and started to make a cup of coffee.

'Well?'

'Well what?'

'Are you going to speak to him?'

'No, I'm not. You've got a chip on your shoulder and act as if you're here on sufferance. You need to grow up. We've got a baby, that's what you wanted. I've done my best to provide for us. I've paid for your daughters to come over twice a year. Now you're back at work, you're in a black cloud most of the time. Dad was right. He said, "Why did you marry a complicated woman and make life hard for yourself? As if you didn't go through enough in your first marriage."'

Our argument went on and quickly became a fight. He stood facing me, yelling, and I stood silent, knowing anything I said would just anger him more. I turned away and walked to our bedroom. He followed me, still yelling. I told him to get out and leave me alone. He pushed me down on the bed and crouched over me, his hands around my neck.

I pushed his chest away and said, 'Get off me, you fool.'

He collapsed and walked out. I think he slept in the living room that night and when I got up in the morning, he had already gone to work. At the time he was on top of me, I felt little, just scorn. I wasn't afraid of him. I knew I was stronger than him, not physically, but emotionally. Perhaps that is why he would lose his temper with me, because I stood up to him. If I were afraid of him, I might have tried to leave him after this. But I had a small hope that he would change and learn to control his temper.

Mostly, when he lost his temper, he would come to me the next day with some gesture of apology, like a bunch of flowers. I kept forgiving him because I didn't know what else to do. I wanted us to have a marriage that worked. To leave him would be to admit failure.

He hasn't attacked me physically since that time, but I know his anger is still there below the surface, and every now and then, it breaks through over something trivial. I try to talk to him about it and his response makes me realise he has little awareness of how his anger affects others.

'Your trouble is you're afraid of conflict. Everyone gets angry, it's a healthy thing. You want things to be nice all the time. This is real life. Grow up.'

He tells me that his father had taught him to be careful around his mother, who went through a very difficult menopause and would collapse with migraines and retreat to her room if anyone in the house raised their voice. He's always repressed his anger, it seems, unable to express it in safe ways. It is like a beast within him that he can't control once the lid is lifted. I hope that he will even out as Sebastian grows older and is less demanding, and if I get onto more of an even keel at work. I know that the anger is bigger than the reasons that brought it to the surface.

One day, he yells at Penelope for something trivial and I make up my mind. I don't want to live with him if it's like this. I don't want her to live in a family where there is conflict and fear of angry eruptions. I want her to have a happy, safe family life, to be supported as she grows into a young woman. She doesn't deserve this after her miserable childhood.

Michael has been going to a psychodrama group once a week. One night he comes home late and climbs into bed beside me.

'How was the group?'

'Oh, good. We had a couple of drinks and a dance afterwards.'

'Ah, is that why I can smell perfume on you?'

He turns away and soon falls asleep.

A friend at work told me that her friend is a member of that group and had mentioned Michael to her. She wondered if there was an affair brewing there. I didn't feel much when she told me that, as Michael and I have been semi-platonic for some time. My stress and his moods have reduced our relationship to one of habit and duty and strained tolerance, with occasional ruptures and releases. Our lovemaking is infrequent, usually after a couple of glasses of wine, and I tend to avoid it if I can. I think that's a big part of why he is angry with me. He told me that when we met again and started our courtship, he imagined that our sex life would be amazing. For him, desire is easily kindled by a touch, a look. For me, it is a will o' the wisp. I need intimate time, shared conversation, laughter, a slow circling around each other until we come close and connect.

One of the things I find difficult is that he is often withdrawn and inexpressive. When we break through that and get close, for him, it always turns into physical desire, and its expression is often painful for me. In lovemaking, he is passionate, but in daily life, he is only emotional when he loses his temper.

What I yearn for is a soulmate. Someone I can talk to or just be with without having to explain or justify why I think the way I do. Someone who may see things differently but who can accept my way of seeing and not judge me for it. Someone who loves me just as I am and doesn't want to shape me. Who doesn't just release his feelings through sex and keep them bottled up the rest of the time.

Perhaps what Michael is seeking is someone who loves him without needing him to express it in words, as I do. He needs lovemaking, penetration, ecstasy, the experience of leaving his body and floating in a universe of colour and shape. He always has psychedelic visions after orgasm. I don't orgasm. In fact, I don't think I ever have, except once when a lover I had persuaded me to take LSD. I need words, tenderness, talking about our feelings. He finds that difficult and closes off.

After his night out, I wait for a day or two and then ask him to sit with me outside in the garden. 'Michael, I feel our relationship has stagnated, it hasn't grown. I don't feel connected to you any more. We're just going through the motions. It's not what I came over here for.'

I look at him and he looks away.

'I want to live separately.'

He stares out across the fence at the surrounding bushland.

'What do you think?' I ask.

'Ah, I don't know what I think. I just know that this life we've created is not what we wanted. I don't know how to change it. I feel I've lost you.'

I think back on the last four years. I hoped that having a child would complete our relationship, would bring him fulfilment, and that the hole in my heart would be sutured and healed. I hoped my lost motherhood would be restored and we would have our own family. I think he hoped for that too, for me and for him. Yet here we are, strangers living together and sharing a bed, with separate desires and fears.

Neither of us has been unfaithful, technically. I know that. But I've had crushes on a couple of men at work. The psychiatrist who cross-examined me when his patient got herself decapitated was my bête noire for a while. He is of average height, with curly brown hair and a hooked nose. He always wears crumpled suits, and we call him Wrinkly. But he is fiercely intelligent and cares deeply for his patients, which I guess is why he gave us such a hard time when that poor girl put her head on the train line. Gradually, he and I became friends, and I found myself looking forward to seeing him. He supported my attempts to change the culture of the unit and find ways for nursing staff to develop their counselling skills.

One night, to my surprise, I dreamed about him, a very explicit sexual dream. He began to occupy my thoughts a lot, and I had more dreams. One day, I asked him if I could have a private chat with him.

I sat opposite him in the chair that his patients usually sit in.

He looked at me, his head tilted a little to one side. 'What is it, Anna?'

'I… I've had some dreams about you lately. I can't get you out of my head. I wonder if you would like to…'

'See you outside of work?'

'Yes.'

'Well, I really appreciate you telling me.' He smiles and his face softens. 'But it wouldn't work for me. I'm already in a relationship.'

'Ah, I wasn't sure. I'm married. But our marriage isn't working. It never has really.'

'You know, Anna, we are like waterholes in the desert. You are different from the other nurses. You think differently, you question things. You are an idealist, I think…you want to make things better. I like talking to you. It's like drinking from the waterhole and being refreshed. Then we have to move on.'

When he said, 'You want to make things better,' it struck a chord. I remember having an appraisal with the sister who was admin for our area.

She sat and looked at me as if she wasn't sure what to say. Then she folded up the form I'd filled out and said, 'The trouble with you, nurse, is that you want to make things better. And that gives us the woops!'

I was surprised by her frankness. 'You know,' I said, 'it wasn't easy for me taking over charge nurse, for many reasons. Not least that the staff have resisted many of my efforts to enable better communication between nurses and doctors, with patients, with families, with the rest of the hospital.' I was thinking of my latest run-in with admin, which brought me up against a brick wall again.

She had no useful advice for me. 'We have priorities you don't understand. Your unit is not the centre of the world.'

The conversation ended there.

I'd put in a proposal for a psychiatric liaison service with other wards like intensive care and accident and emergency because they often have patients who are mentally and emotionally disturbed, sometimes psychotic, and they have no training in how to deal with them.

When I put the proposal to the director of nursing, she heard me out but turned me down. I asked her why.

'Nurse, you must accept that this is a big, busy hospital and our funds are stretched. We don't have the resources to give you the staffing and the time from normal duties to make this work.'

'But we can rearrange our hours to fit it in. The outpatients sister is very interested in doing this work. He's very approachable and easy to communicate with, as well as knowledgeable. He's willing to do some training in his own time and take on the role. There are times when there's not much for him to do over there, and we can cover for him.'

'I've made it clear that we can't agree to it.' She sat back in her chair and looked at me, her mouth folded in a tight line. 'You have an abrasive manner! Please take this as a firm no.'

Maybe trying to make things better is my problem. I don't want to accept things as they are. I question why they must be so, and others resist that.

I had thought perhaps I'd found a kindred soul in the wrinkly doctor. Maybe I had, but he wasn't an escape route. After that, I was able to let go of him in my thoughts and accept the attraction for what it was...a kinship between two strangers who meet within the limits of work. But it made me realise that Michael isn't able to give me the deep sense of connection I crave.

In the garden, after I've broached the subject of separating, Michael walks across to the gate that leads out into the bushland.

'I'm going for a walk. If you want to separate, it's up to you. You'll take Sebastian with you, of course, because I can't look after him on my own. You'll have to find somewhere to rent. Let's give it six months and see how we feel then. I'll keep up the mortgage repayments, but you'll have to pay your own rent.'

I hadn't really considered the practicalities. It would be much easier for me if he moved out and I stayed on here with Penelope and Sebastian. But since I am the one wanting the separation, I won't pick a fight over it.

I wonder if we should have separated after I first came over here, once I realised I'd made a mistake. If I'd gone back to Sydney, at least I'd be near my family. But we wouldn't have had Sebastian. Now we share a child, I'll have to stay here and make the best of things.

Twelve

I find a three-bedroom house in a beach suburb, about ten minutes' drive from our house. It happens to be opposite Penelope's piano teacher, who is a friend of Michael's.

Penelope, or Penny, as I often call her now, longed to play the piano when she was little, but her stepmother discouraged her. Kate said the noise of her playing the scales and exercises drove her mad. She stopped Robert from paying for her lessons.

When Penny came to live with us, I searched for a teacher, and once she started lessons, I advertised in the paper for a kind person who would let her practise on their piano. We found one living in the same suburb and were amused and surprised to find he was a friend of David Helfgott. My dream is to buy her a piano.

She isn't happy at the big high school in Scarborough. A mob of surfie girls bully her and, although she stands up to them, she finds it stressful. I don't want her to have more stress in her life. I want her to feel safe and happy. I talk to her piano teacher about it, and she tells me of a couple of high schools in the northern suburbs that have special music programs. Penny and I decide on the one that is further away because it has a reputation for offering lots of choice and graduating many students who go on to thrive in their professions. Perth Modern is in North Perth, near the railway line. We work out that Penny can catch a bus to the train station and get a train to school, a trip of forty-five minutes with the right connections. She is to start there in the first term of next year, her sixteenth year. We will hire musical instruments for her after she decides which ones she wants to specialise in.

Once I decide to separate from Michael, I give up working in inpatients in the psych ward. It's bad enough for Sebastian to lose one parent in his daily life without losing two of us. So, after a few months of working back in outpatients, where I can do daytime shifts, I hand in my resignation and look for part-time, casual work in the community as a frail aged carer. Sebastian will start preschool next year, which will make it easier. Meantime, I still have to take him to day care.

Michael drops in whenever he can, usually without notice. I'm not happy with the way he treats our rented house as if it were his own, but I want him to be able to see Sebastian. We don't have a formal separation agreement. Michael is paying day care fees and a small allowance towards other costs. If I try to regulate his visits or ask for notice, he might withdraw that support.

He buys Sebastian a two-wheeler with trainer wheels for his birthday, and Penny spends lots of time with Sebastian in the back lane, running behind him with her hands on the seat. She lets go a few times and he overbalances and falls off. Each time, he gets back on and they start again.

One afternoon, I'm standing at the gate watching. She shoots me a

smile and lets go, but keeps running behind him. He pedals on, gripping the handles. Then he turns to check on her and overbalances.

'See, Pod, you did it!'

He rages at her for letting go and she laughs and explains that he's ridden about three metres without her holding on. She hugs him and they fall over on a tuft of grass, laughing.

Before Michael and I separated, I'd begun searching for a spiritual meaning to my life. My dream of marriage and a family hadn't turned out as I hoped. I stopped going to the Satyananda ashram after Sebastian was born. I missed it and I wanted something to replace it. I felt tense all the time and wanted to become centred, more in tune with my body.

I began having massages with a woman called Rose. She is Dutch Indonesian, in her sixties, with silver hair and a strong accent. She says that she can see spots in the body where there is illness or imbalance.

'What can you see?' I say, as she presses her hands under my breasts and began to move them down in semicircular strokes over my upper abdomen.

'Your heart…it is stressed.'

'Does that mean I have heart disease?'

'No. It is locked up, it wants to be more open, to let more love in, to give more love out.'

'Oh, I don't know, Rose. I thought my life would be happy once I had a child to bring up, to love without losing.'

'So what do you lack?'

'Ah, I miss Sydney. I miss my family. I've never felt at home here.'

'What would make it more like home for you?'

'Well, I was unhappy and angry before I had Sebastian. Then I fell in love with that little baby, but I had to go back to work. It was a struggle, first night duty, then shift work, having to leave Sebastian with carers. Michael and I grew further apart. I thought I'd be happy when Penelope came to live with us. I thought we could create a happy family 'life together.

'Has she settled in?'

'It's hard for her too. We haven't lived together since she was two, and naturally, it will take time to build trust between us. But it was harder when we were living with Michael…that undercurrent of tension, me trying to avoid conflict with him, wanting to protect her.'

Rose cups my right foot in one hand and presses her thumb in firmly under the ball of my right foot. I gasp.

'Hmm. Lots of stress there, built up in your adrenals. You are under a lot of pressure, and you feel alone.'

I start to cry. She passes me a tissue, then moves to the other foot and works on it. Gradually, I feel a softening in my abdomen.

'That's good. It's good to cry, let the feelings out.'

'When Penny came over, I was so anxious for her to have a happy family life, to be free to be herself, not to have to hide and try to be good so she wouldn't be punished.'

'And have you been able to give her that?'

'I've tried really hard, but work and all the stress on top of Michael's moods have made it difficult.'

'What is lacking in your life?' Her hands are stroking my feet from toe to heel, around the ankles, then lightly up towards the knees.

'An equal love with a man. But I've just about given up on that. I haven't found it with Michael.'

'What else?' Her hands sweep from my knees up to my groin, then softly swirl around my abdomen.

'Something to believe in. Some meaning outside human love and work…a connection beyond life and death and whatever else there is.'

She moves up to my head and presses on points from my forehead to the crown. Then around the temples and down to the nape of the neck. I feel tension sliding out under her hands and my jaw softens.

'There, Anna,' she says as she covers me with warm towels. 'Lie there and relax for a few minutes. When you're ready, get dressed and come into the office and we'll have a chat.'

Sitting in her cosy office, I let my eyes rest on the batik print hanging on the wall. She comes in with a ceramic tray bearing a matching pot and two squat clay cups. I love this ritual, the way she elegantly pours the tea from the pot held high above the cup, the music the tea makes as it meets the cup. I inhale the sweet smell of jasmine as I sip the green tea.

'Anna, have you heard of the Centre?'

'No, what is it?'

'Its other name is the Church of the Mystic Christ. Mario Schoenmaker is the founder and director. He is a gifted clairvoyant. He read my aura and the Akashic records and told me about past incarnations. It made so much sense, why my life has been like it has. It gave me a new lease of life.'

'What are the Akashic records?'

'A man called Edgar Cayce introduced them to us early in the twentieth century. They're a vast database of all that has happened, is happening and will happen in all the universes together. Once, only mystics, saints and scholars knew about them. But they have been revealed to us now so we can know that we are infinite beings in a reality of many dimensions. These bodies –' she strikes her chest, 'are not all we are.'

'What do you need to do to get a reading?'

'I can take you along to a service and introduce you. Then he'll make a time to do the reading.'

Thirteen

Mario has gone back to Melbourne, where the Centre began. Robert is the priest in charge now, a tall man with a reserved manner and a quiet energy. His offsiders are Claire and Christopher. Christopher has a heavenly voice, and when he sings songs like 'The Rose', it brings tears to my eyes. Penny comes to services with me and loves the rituals and the singing. We are both in love with Christopher and his voice.

Claire and I become good friends after she does a tarot reading for me. Her husband died of brain cancer. Now, she and Christopher are lovers, but she keeps a jealous eye on him, because most of the women in the church are infatuated with him, and he enjoys their adoration.

The teachings are based on esoteric scriptures that Robert says have been hidden and suppressed since the death of Christ, and on revelations Mario has had from the Akashic records. The mission of the church is to introduce us to that source and help us to cultivate our personal sacred relationship with the true reality. The aim is that our daily lives, where we work, sleep, eat and love, are connected to a source of knowledge that is infinite and timeless.

We go to weekly meetings where we share tea and coffee and cakes made by some of the members and ask questions about the teachings and how they can guide us in our daily lives.

I decide to be initiated, which involves studying some of the sacred texts, discussing them with Robert, and attending a special service where I am blessed. I receive a silver cross engraved with a rose symbolising the mystic Christ.

Michael comes along to my initiation. I ask him why and he says, 'Because I know it means a lot to you.' There is a sting to this tail. I think he is very suspicious of the Centre and its teachings and wants to find out more about it. I tell him that one of the members wants to set up a community in the hills, where families and individuals live together, grow organic fruit and vegetables, and share services.

'Do you want to be part of it?'

'Yes, I do. It makes sense to share resources with like-minded people, instead of living separately.'

'I don't want you to take Sebastian into a set-up like that. I don't want him in a cult. Next thing, they'll be wanting money contributions and maybe more than that. And indoctrinating the children.'

'Michael, it's not a cult. It's a community of like-minded people who want to live a more connected life, sharing resources and services and studying ways of living a better life.'

'Rubbish! It's based on a deranged ratbag's balderdash concocted from a few suspect texts. It's a way of brainwashing people into giving their energy and resources to profit the guys who lead it. And brainwashing their kids. If you try to go and live up there, I'll take you to court.'

I can see he is very afraid of losing Sebastian, perhaps of losing me. We have had many arguments about whether there is anything beyond this mortal life. He is an atheist and there is an emotional charge to his arguments against mysticism. I wonder if he was an alchemist, a healer or a mystic in a former life, failed in his quest to turn base metals into gold. Perhaps he was persecuted for his beliefs, or his practice as an apothecary. He has two tall glass flasks that used to be the trademark of the pharmacist's trade. He has one filled with ruby-red water and one with emerald-green. The only part of his work he still enjoys is making up liniments, cough mixtures or tonics for people who are searching for a cure for some chronic condition.

The community idea doesn't become a reality, but Claire tells me about a house in Victoria Park which is owned by a couple who are Centre members and are moving to Melbourne to study with Mario. 'It's a lovely, light-filled house. Two bedrooms with a sleepout. It would be perfect for you and your little family.'

The rent is affordable and the bus to town stops in the street, so Penny can catch a bus into town and a short train trip to the school. We move in before she starts school at Perth Modern.

Fourteen

Claire and Christopher decide to move to Melbourne too, to join with Mario in developing the Centre there.

Claire has a proposition to make to me. 'You know I make a living by doing waxing. It's called Meticulous Waxing. Well, I'd like to offer you the agency here. It's the sole agency in Perth with a superior wax developed by a woman at the Centre in Melbourne. You can pay me off on a monthly basis.'

'I don't know, Claire. I've never done anything like that. Is it difficult to learn?'

'No, you just have to get the knack of it. I can give you lessons. And I'll include all the stock I have in the price.'

I swallow my doubts and start having lessons. It could give me a way of working from home while Sebastian is little. As my office, I use one of the front rooms in the house, the one that was my bedroom, and sleep in the living room.

Claire shows me how to clean the leg surface first and apply a little baby powder to soak up any oil in the skin. 'When the wax in the pot is the right temperature, you dip the paddle in and shake off excess, smooth it on the leg in the direction the hair grows. Then, take a cotton pad and smooth it over the waxed skin in a downward motion. The tricky part is pulling the pad off. You pull it against the direction of the hair growth, in a sharp, clean movement. At the same time, put your other hand on the leg below where you've applied the wax and hold it firm. That way, you create a stabilising force the other hand pulls against, so that the wax comes off cleanly with the hairs, and it doesn't drag on the skin below it. When you get the trick of it, the client will feel a brief pulling sensation but no pain. More like a tickle spread out over the length of the pad.'

I practise and practise, on me, on Claire, on Penny, until Claire says I'm ready to treat my first client. I get some flyers printed with a half-price offer and take them to shopping centres. It's hard work and I find it very confronting to approach people and offer them something they probably know nothing about and may not want. I end up leaving a few flyers on tables in the shared spaces and putting some up on notice boards. I also put a weekly ad in the local paper.

A few people respond, and I start to feel a bit more confident.

I train Sebastian to answer the phone when I'm busy. His take on this is ''Ello, Metic-lious Waxing!'

One day he hands me the phone and says, 'It's a man, Mum!'

He rings back several times and though I refuse him each time, eventually I give in and make a time.

He is lying on the couch, sweating. He's removed his trousers and is wearing women's underpants. They are grubby with lacy edges. His legs are coated in thick, strong hairs. As I stand with my back to him stirring the wax, I psych myself into doing this. Maybe he's a cross-dresser and that's why he wants his legs waxed. He has a right to that.

But the first waxing leaves a lot of hairs behind. I reapply the wax twice, until I've removed most of them, then go over with the tweezers to pull out strays. I put lots of soothing lotion on afterwards. It takes me nearly an hour, all for half price, twelve dollars. As I see him out the door, I resolve not to treat any more men.

Soon after I start the waxing business, I have a visitation. I sleep on a mattress in the living room, on the raised half of the floor. One morning when it's still dark, I wake up and my eyes are drawn to the far window. There's enough reflected light from the street to see there's a gap between the edge of the curtain and the window frame. In that gap, I see a girl's face staring at me. She is deathly pale, with a mass of dark hair and eyes ringed with kohl. Blood is oozing from the corner of her mouth. I am transfixed and hold her stare for a few minutes. Gradually, she fades away.

Heart thumping, I jump out of bed and check on the children. Penny is sound asleep in the front bedroom and Sebastian in his bunk bed in the sleepout behind the dining room. The doors are locked and all is quiet.

I phone Claire and talk to her about it. What does she think it was? A ghost, a haunting? I didn't know the face, but it reminded me of Caitlin, who is now living in London. Penny had visited England with her father the previous Christmas, before she came to live with me. She returned to tell me that Caitlin is a heroin addict and a street prostitute. I was not really surprised, for I knew that when she left home at the age of sixteen, she was living in the fast lane, taking speed and other drugs. She and her boyfriend went to England via Thailand and she wrote me long, rambling letters and poems. I had lost her and didn't know if she would ever return.

I lost her trust when she was eleven years old and wanted to stay with me in Sydney rather than go back with her sisters to Melbourne, to her father and stepfamily. My lawyer and my brother told me I couldn't keep her. If she wanted to be with me, there would first have to be a genuine attempt to resolve family conflict and problems, and if that didn't happen, she and her sisters would have to testify in court that they were being abused. I had no choice but to send her back. After that, when I was living in Perth with Michael, I knew she was lost and unhappy and in a permanent state of rebellion in her stepfamily.

I asked her several times if she wanted to come and live with me and Michael. If she did, I said, I would make sure it happened.

She replied, 'Mum, I can't. I can't leave Dad. I would be a better person if I came and lived with you, but he needs me here and I will stay as long as I can.'

Later, she told me that when she went back to Melbourne that time after she'd tried to stay with me, she told him how Kate was treating her and Penny, her cruelty, her injustice, and how she hated her and hated her step-siblings. Her father had sobbed on her shoulder and told her that if she left him, he would die.

He was the ultimate narcissist, a man who took his children away from me because he wanted to punish me, their mother, and because he believed he couldn't live without them. A man who kept them with him even though he knew they were being treated cruelly. His was a subtle, selfish cruelty. Kate's was volatile and unpredictable. She was jealous of his love for them and harsh to them when he was not around, which was often. She would be affectionate and playful some of the time, but they never knew when she would turn on them. The household was a hierarchy, run like an army, with him as the absent major, visiting occasionally, with very little idea what went on in his absence, and her as the captain. Her own children were her favourites and, like Cinderella, my girls were made to do more chores than her children and were punished when they did things wrong or forgot to do things. The girls told me that she and Robert quarrelled a lot, she expressing resentment over his workaholic habits and frequent trips away, he justifying his life as a leading scientist in his field and insisting that he needed her support.

Penelope, as the youngest, was at the bottom of the heap. Caitlin had protected her as much as she could and resisted Kate's tyranny until she was old enough to escape. She was a fighter and a rebel and defied her stepmother's attempts to control her.

Sophia had been drawn into complex entanglements with her stepsister and -brother, and had distanced herself from her own sisters and father to protect herself and appease her stepfamily. In her gentle and sensitive nature, she avoided conflict as much as she could. She left home as soon as she finished school.

That left Penelope caught between her father's clinging love and her stepmother's jealous surveillance and control. I'm so glad she has escaped that.

As for the ghost, I don't know what it meant. Perhaps it was the spirit of a girl who died here, trapped in this place, lost. I believe that

if people die in unhappy circumstances, or unexpectedly, their spirits are not able to leave this earthly sphere and move to a higher plane. They haunt the spaces they lived or died in.

Or perhaps it was Caitlin's soul calling for help, wanting to reunite with me. I burn candles at night when I go to bed, I sprinkle salt around the room, I pray for protection. The apparition hasn't returned. But sometimes I wake with a start, feeling that a net is being thrown over me. Or I see a child leaping across the room when I open my eyes, and I can't go back to sleep.

I keep the business going for a few months, but I'm not making much money from it, and it's hard to find the monthly payments for Claire. I decide to sell the agency if I can. Meticulous is big in Melbourne, but I'm not the one to make it a success here. I write to Claire and tell her I can't keep doing it. I've paid off about half the price she asked for, and I explain I'm not making it work and can't keep paying her. If I can sell it, I will pay her the rest. She doesn't answer. And so, our financial arrangement, my waxing experiment and our friendship come to an end.

Not long after, we stop going to the Centre. Sebastian doesn't want to go any more, Penny is getting into the swing of social and music life with her friends at Perth Modern, and I haven't found what I was looking for.

I realise that my friendships at the Centre meant more to me than the teachings, and now Claire and Christopher are gone, it feels empty to me. I don't want a sense of the divine as separate, encased in teachings and rituals and esoteric lore. I want to feel the divine saturated in everyday life, in the earth, in the sky, the wind and the water…in me, in you, everywhere, in everything. The Centre hasn't given me that. It seems like a latter-day version of the church that framed my school life, with teachings and preachings and prayers and people who profess to be holy, messengers of god, separate, external to the self. I don't want religion. Religion separates people from the creator, the source of life.

When Sebastian was about three, I asked him what he thought god was. He thought for a minute and said, 'I think god's us.'

These years as a single parent when Sebastian is little and Penny is at school are graced with many pleasures. Living in this simple weatherboard and fibro house with the big overgrown backyard, keeping bantam hens who manage to escape their enclosure and lay their eggs in secret caches, surprising a hen running out from a bush with a train of little chicks behind her.

The street we live in sweeps down a hill and up again to the west, and it feels old. The houses are mostly weatherboard or plasterboard and fibro on quarter-acre blocks, like ours. They haven't been replaced by blocks of units or Macmansions as in the newer suburbs. In the streets down near the river, there are still a lot of brick Federation-style houses with gables and bay windows. When I walk out onto the veranda at night, I hear the wind sighing in the pine trees at the west end of the street and feel a sense of peace and acceptance. It's not easy being a single parent with a teenager and a five-year-old, but it's more peaceful than living in a marriage that is not working.

Sebastian goes to the primary school down the hill near the river. On the first morning of school term, I walk down with him and he rides his bicycle. I don't realise until I meet him after school that he will have to ride his bike uphill. We get about halfway when he refuses to ride any further.

I hail a bus.

The driver says, 'Ah sorry, lady, no bikes!'

'Please,' I say, smiling as sweetly as I can. 'It's my son's first day at school and he can't ride his bike up the hill.'

'Orright, where're ya goin?'

'Sussex Street, thanks so much.'

For Penny's fifteenth birthday, she has her first sleepover since she came to live with me. About eight of her friends from Perth Mod, girls and boys, sit and lounge around the two levels of the living room, listening to music, laughing and talking, loud and happy. I've cooked up big pots of bolognese and spaghetti. Sebastian has his friend from school over for the night too, so he doesn't feel left out. After clearing up the kitchen, I read to the little boys and tuck them into bed.

My bedroom adjoins the living room. I don't get much sleep. Their noise goes on till the early hours of the morning. I should have slept in Penny's room for the night but can't be bothered moving. I bang on the wall a few times and call, 'I can't sleep!' It makes no difference. Around dawn, they quieten down and I catch a couple of hours.

It is interesting, helping Penny navigate her turbulent teenage years, her first romance, her heartbreaks, her friendships. It seems natural to me that she should be free to experiment, to express herself, to find her own path. I didn't have that freedom. I was sent away to boarding school by my mother when I was thirteen, dressed up like a parcel in school uniform, surrounded by rules and routines. Penny spent twelve years of her life in a regimented, abusive family where she was the littlest, the one most picked on. I want her to grow into adulthood without those bonds around her.

I feel guilty that I'm not more involved in her school life. Some of her friends' parents are on committees, organising functions, running fund-raising raffles. I don't have the resources to do so. I'm on supporting parents' benefit and earn a little extra by helping at the creche run by the council at the shopping centre. I earn $3 an hour. Parents can leave their infants there for a couple of hours while they do their shopping or have medical appointments. I spend most of my time holding crying babies or toddlers, trying to console them, to help them feel safe. It mirrors all the times I held my own daughters when they cried at the airport, when I had to hand them over to the hostess and watch them walk across the tarmac to the plane. All the times I wanted to be with them and hold them and could not. Perhaps there is healing in it for me. I hope at least there is consolation for them.

I try network marketing with a cosmetics and skin care company called Nutrimetics. I put flyers around and hand them out to shoppers. As with the half-price waxing offers, I find it soul-destroying and don't have the heart to try and build an income from it, so I give it up. Another failed experiment.

We managed to sell the house in the northern suburbs after it had been with an agent for three months. The agent, one of Michael's golfing friends, had done nothing with it. He thought it was hard to sell because it was in an estate and had strata title – not a 'proper' house.

I said, 'I'll sell it.'

I was still going to the Centre then and I got Christopher, who did house painting to support himself, to paint the rooms for me. I advertised it as a private sale and sold it within a fortnight. My share of the sale price went towards paying off my overdraft. But it grew again! Debt is a condition I live with, the price of being single. Then again, Michael has always lived with debt and juggled earnings against the costs of keeping a wife and children.

When Mum died, she left some money to me and my brothers. My share came to about thirty thousand. Michael said to me, 'What's mine is yours and what's yours is mine.' I didn't want to put it into paying off some of the mortgage, as he suggested, and decided to spend it. I bought a new Mazda, the first new car I'd had, gave some money to each of my daughters and to Michael's two daughters, some to him to buy some new clothes, and some for myself.

Now, my debt is increasing again and I don't earn enough to pay it off. I don't want to sell the Mazda. It is associated with Mum for me, but I have to get rid of my debt. I shed a few tears. To compensate and fulfil a dream, I use some of the money to buy Penny a piano.

When I go round the supermarket, I have a panic attack. Can I make the money stretch to buy all we need? The gas and electricity bills come in and I don't have enough to pay them, so I go to Social Services and ask for a handout. Michael gives me some money towards the rent, but each week is a struggle.

A year has gone by. It's 1986, Sebastian is turning six in December, Penny will be in her final year at Perth Mod next year, and Michael has asked me to come back to him. I visit him with Sebastian in the flat he's taken near the beach at Sorrento. We spend an evening and a night together and he tells me he still loves me.

For me, nothing has changed. I feel the same ambivalence towards him. There is much I love about him…his brown eyes, his slim body, his voice, his love of poetry, his wit, his intuition. He is a good listener, except when challenged. Then he can switch into attack mode. And sometimes, I can't help challenging him, as we have such different beliefs.

He respects authority and often says, 'Well, if so and so says this is how it has to be, they must know what they're talking about.'

'Why must they?' I ask. 'Germans did what Hitler told them to do because they believed he knew what he was talking about.'

'Oh, you always twist an argument.'

I know he loves me and he dearly loves and misses Sebastian. He wants to reunite so he can have his family back.

Our family is split into two jagged parts. The patterns of the puzzle are askew because we want different things. He wants stability and security and the solace of sex and companionship and a child. I want meaning and shared values and change, not the staleness of habit and the known.

We married, we had a child, a much-loved son, but we can't quite make the parts fit together. When the four of us are together, there's an awkwardness. Perhaps it's always like this with blended families.

Next time I visit him, we talk about living together again.

'I could come and live at Vic Park with you guys, so we'd only be paying one lot of rent.'

'Is that the only reason?'

'No, of course not. But it's a consideration.

'Not very romantic! Why do you want to live with us again?'

'Well, we're still married. I still love you. I want to have a family life.'

'Hmmm. I don't know. I want to see Penny through her school year, and I want her life to be stable and peaceful. She needs that.'

'Do you mean you choose her rather than me?'

'No, I mean that I lost her when she was an infant and it's really important that I give her this time in a family where she feels safe and accepted and free to become the person she wants to be. She lost her childhood because of the choices Robert and I made and she had a miserable time. This is her time.'

'So I come second?'

Really, you come third. There's Penny and there's Sebastian. A fragile family, but it works and I don't want to stress it. It's a balancing act, parenting a six-year-old and a sixteen-year-old-becoming-a-woman, all the while trying to survive on less than a living wage. Yet I want Sebastian to have time with his dad for however long that's possible. I want him to have as normal a childhood as possible.

Nothing's been normal in my life since my father left. I fear abandonment and my defence is to separate from someone if I don't feel safe with them. I stopped being lovers with my lawyer because I knew he would never commit to sharing his life with me. I left my life in Sydney because I hoped that Michael and I could build a life together. When it wasn't working, I left him. It didn't work before. Can it ever work?

I've always felt out of place, having to fit in, trying to please and be what I'm expected to be. I thought marriage to Michael would bring normality and greater ease, but it hasn't. At times it feels like a mirage, that shimmering illusion of water beyond the flat, dry plains, hovering on the horizon, disappearing as you get near it.

'I don't know, Michael. First, second, third…it doesn't mean anything. There's no order in my life, no symmetry. Any order I've ever had was imposed on me. Now, I'm just trying to make do, to improvise, to at least give Penny some home life till she's ready to take flight, and to give Sebastian the love and security he needs.'

'Then let me help you.' He rests his palm in my hand, as he used to when he courted me, and gazes at me – brown eyes, often blinking and looking away, now steady and limpid.

'Oh, let me sleep on it.'

We have a couple more glasses of wine while Sebastian builds a castle with the Lego that Michael keeps for him to play with.

I look at the clock. 'Oh, it's late. I'll put Sebastian to bed.'

I tuck him into the spare bed and Michael comes and tells him a story, another adventure in the life of Bilbo the bilby who gets lost in the bush and tries to find his way home, meeting interesting characters along the way.

When Michael kisses him and says goodnight, Sebastian struggles out of bed and runs back to his Lego set. Michael calls him and Sebastian ignores him. This tussle goes on for a while, until Michael loses his temper and kicks him. Sebastian bursts into tears and I pick him up.

'There, darling. You're OK. I'll take you home.'

I glare at Michael and pick up my bag. As I drive home, Sebastian sobs himself to sleep in the car seat.

It won't work, getting back together again. I don't trust Michael.

Next day, Michael comes to visit me while Sebastian is at school. I'm still angry with him. Hurting Sebastian isn't something I can just let go.

'How could you do that? How could you kick your little boy?'

'I…don't know. It just happened.'

'It just happened? Nothing ever just happens. You made it happen.'

'He wouldn't stay in bed! It was late.'

'You lost your temper because you wanted to have sex with me and Sebastian was in the way.'

'And you're so superior! You never lose your temper, you're a perfect mother.' His voice is rising.

'I think you should go, Michael. This conversation's going nowhere.'

I turn away from him and he steps up and kicks me as I bend over to pick up some pieces of Sebastian's Lego on the floor. I fall on my hand and knees and crawl over to the wall, where I sit down, hugging my knees, crying. 'Just go!'

He walks out.

A few days later, we talk about what happened. He is contrite, acknowledges that what he did was wrong and promises it won't happen again.

I am sceptical. I know Sebastian has forgiven him, perhaps even forgotten it happened, and will keep his loving heart open. But I think there will be more clashes between us because I am not afraid of his temper, even though I disrespect him for not being able to control it. I am afraid he will take his bad moods out on Sebastian. I don't want Sebastian to grow up afraid of his father.

Even so, I'm aware that I provoke him by challenging his opinions and beliefs. Some of our most heated arguments have been about politics (he is conservative, I am left wing) and doctrines he holds about medicine and food. He loves sweet things and carbohydrates; I avoid sugar and think he uses far too much salt. He thinks that medication is life-saving, medical science is a wonder of the modern age and doctors' advice should be always be followed. After years in mental health nursing, I am sceptical about the medical model and have seen too many mistakes and even malpractice to think that the doctor always knows best. There is far too much over-prescription and too many invasive tests and procedures. In my childhood in the outback, we used poultices and inhalations for infections and inflammations, and a trip to the doctor or to hospital was rare. We will never agree on these things. I need to stop waving the red flag at the bull and provoking him.

After a few days of soul-searching, I decide to give him another chance to make a family with us. I talk to Penelope about it first, and she agrees. She is happy in her school and with her friends and loves having a little brother. She loves Michael and seems to accept his moodiness.

He visits again and after Sebastian is asleep and Penny has gone out to a movie with her friends, we sit on the veranda, sipping a glass of cool wine after a hot day.

'Michael, I'm ready to try living together again, if you still want to.'
'Of course I do.'
'There's a couple of things I need to share. I can't accept physical punishment of a child. My mother used to pull my pants down and smack me when I was naughty. I felt ashamed and humiliated. It's no way to teach a child.'

'Ah, I agree with you. I've never done that before and it won't happen again. I lost my temper, I was tired. I was wrong. I'll tell him I'm sorry about it.'

'OK. There's one other thing. Penny – she's a young woman now. She is enjoying school and her friends, her music. She needs to be happy and feel safe. I am a little concerned that you might not agree with the amount of freedom I give her. She has a boyfriend, having her first serious romance. I don't want her to feel watched over and restricted like I did when I was a teenager living with my mother. I have an open, trusting relationship with her. I hope you will be able to share that and respect her freedom to explore life and express herself.'

'I love her too, and I think she's a fine young woman. I agree, she needs space to find herself and I respect the way you've been parenting her.'

We agree then. He says he will give notice to his landlord and move in as soon as he can.

I go back to sleeping in the living room and he sleeps in my bedroom. I don't feel ready to sleep with him again. I want to see how we get along first.

We rumble along okay. Now he's here, sharing the parenting with me, I go back to psych nursing. I take a job in the private psych wing at St John of God Hospital. I know the charge nurse and negotiate with him to do all day shifts. I get up in the mornings about six and put on my uniform. I allow half an hour to get to work. Michael gets up with me and makes me tea and toast. He even fashions a little cardboard carrier so I can eat and drink in the car.

We have a cat called Igor. He was Caitlin's cat in Melbourne, and when she went to England, she sent him over to me in a crate. Poor Igor was so traumatised when I took him to the house that he darted out of my arms and climbed onto the top of the wardrobe in Penny's bedroom. He stayed up there for three days, refusing all enticement to come down. Then he leaped down and shot through the house, out the screen door at the back, disappearing for a day or two. When he returned, he was subdued, but gradually consented to affection and claimed his sleeping place at the foot of Sebastian's bed.

When Michael moved in, Igor was disgruntled. He ignored Michael and refused all his overtures.

One morning, my day off from work, Michael emerged from the bedroom. 'That bloody cat has shat on my bed!'

A bad omen.

Fifteen

Michael and I separated two more times. We had both tried very hard to make it work. I didn't feel that I knew what love was any more. After following him to a country town in WA's Great Southern region, then to another town in the Pilbara, I'd gone back to being a single parent. Then, when Sebastian was in his eleventh year, Michael bought a pharmacy in a wheatbelt town and asked if I would come and live with him there so we could be a family again. I thought about it for a while and said I would, but I wanted to remarry. I'm not sure now why I thought it was a good idea or how it would help us strengthen our relationship. I think I felt the need for a ritual, shared with our family and friends, that would put the seal on what had fallen apart three times. But after eighteen months in the wheatbelt town, I realised, once again, that we couldn't make it work. I moved down to Perth and found a flat, and Sebastian finished the school year living with his father, then returned to me. Together, we moved from one rented flat or house to another and I saw him through the last year of primary school and on to the end of year eleven in high school. He had had six different primary schools, and perhaps that was why he was averse to change and chose to stay in a mainstream high school rather than an alternative one, which I would have preferred.

He was an underachiever and a couch potato, a delightful boy who hid his light under a bushel and kept a low profile. Until he left school and took an apprenticeship. He got interested in martial arts and began to read avidly in this subject. Over two years, I saw him transform on all levels – physical, intellectual, emotional and spiritual. He had never shown any interest in study while he was at school, but once he left, he researched everything he was interested in and became more articulate and confident. I had always given him a lot of rope, for I recognised his strong, independent spirit and knew that if I tried to restrict and discipline him, he would react and go even further down the risky road. It was hard bringing him up on my own, as his father still lived in the wheatbelt, and my daughters were living separate lives. But I knew it would have been harder if Michael was still with us, for he might not have been able to tolerate Sebastian's misadventures and mistakes.

In 1998, Penny, aged twenty-nine, was living in Japan, teaching English, and married to a Japanese man. Sophia had been living in England for a few years and had returned to Western Australia. Now she was married and had two little boys. Caitlin had come back from England, did rehab at a drug and alcohol institute, trained as a youth worker and fell in love with a colleague, Simon. They lived together and had two little boys. Sebastian was going on eighteen, working as a motor mechanic, and I took a job as a relief coordinator for frail aged community care.

I'd worked as a carer for the few years leading to this time, and thought it was a step up, a way to build a career for myself at last. I was working with Joondalup City Council, filling in for someone on maternity leave. There was a lot to learn: protocols, data entry systems, the client needs, what services were available. I soon got the hang of it and enjoyed the days when I could visit clients in their homes to review their services.

There were challenges. One week, our manager told us there was spare money in the budget, so we could give extra services to those who needed them. Next month, she told us the budget was blown and we had to cut back services by at least ten per cent. I had to go back and explain to our clients why they couldn't have that extra help.

The officer I was relieving decided not to come back and the position was advertised. I applied. The day of the interview, I sat at my desk all day, working, trying not to think about what the interview would be like, what questions they'd ask me, who would interview me. They interviewed all the outsiders first. Finally, at five p.m., they called me in. I had to go through two lots of security doors on the ground floor to get to the interview room. My manager and another woman were waiting for me. There was no water jug or glass and they told me to go to the bathroom to get some. Out through the security doors and back in again. It was a bad omen. They were ungracious and uncaring, and I felt unwelcome and unsupported.

I can't remember what questions they asked me, but I was nervous. Yet I felt I should get the position, because I'd done my job well and the clients and other officers liked me.

A week later, I learned they had given the position to someone else.

I asked for feedback. My manager told me the person they'd given the position to was better qualified and had interviewed well. She had a degree in Human Services, apparently. My mental health training and twelve years of experience in community care didn't count.

I was disappointed. Worse, I felt I was at a dead end. What would I do now? Go back to casual work as a carer? I'd started psychotherapy training at the Churchill Centre in Subiaco, but I knew that would take another couple of years to finish, and it was expensive.

Next time I went to the centre, I told the director what had happened.

'You sound a bit depressed. Would you like to have a few sessions with me?'

'I can't afford it.'

'I'll do it half price.'

'OK, thank you.'

In my first session, I sat in his small room, sparsely furnished, with a window looking out onto the courtyard. The building was classical Federation style, built of aged brick, with arched doorways inside and moulded ceilings and skirting boards. There was a feeling of peace and safety within its walls, which were thick and muted the sounds of the outside world.

There was no desk between us, just a small round glass-topped table with a flask of water and two glasses. An old pendulum clock hung on the wall behind us. The delicately-wrought black hands stood at three fifteen. I knew the session would last fifty minutes, so I would hear the clock strike the hour before we finished. I wondered what the chime would be like.

I took a deep breath and looked at him. His kind face and dark eyes that promised he would listen to me and not judge me. I told him the story of my life – my childhood, the loss of my children, my failed second marriage.

The hands of the clock pointed at three fifty. I sat back, my eyes closed, waiting for him to speak. What could he tell me that I didn't already know? It felt good to have been listened to, but I couldn't see how he could help me find a way to live the rest of my life in a more fulfilling way. My life clock had some years to run yet. My son would leave home and make his own life and my daughters each had partners and children, or the prospect of them. What was I to do with the rest of my life? I felt this was a turning point, an arched doorway into a corridor where there were rooms that needed furnishing and living in. I wanted my life to have some shape and elegance, like this lovely building, not to be messy and disjointed, stopping and starting, taking a wrong turn, backing out, starting again.

'Anna,' he said, looking up at the ceiling, then at me, 'it's not your fault. It's the system you were born into.' He talked a little about patriarchy and the failure of men within that system to acknowledge that women are their equals, to engage with them at all levels, from the daily domestic routines to the creative and spiritual levels of life. Worse, he said, was the pattern he saw in many men of not being available in intimate ways other than sexual and perhaps financial, and of walking away, emotionally or physically, when things got hard.

He suggested that I turn my lens around. Instead of seeing the messes and mistakes, as under a microscope, to look through the telescope and see the bigger picture, the repeating patterns and how I had tried to change them. 'When you were a child, what did you give your mother? How would her life have been if she had not had you there? When you lost your children, how would their lives have been if you had cut yourself off from them like your father did? How would Penny have grown into adulthood if you had not given her safety and freedom in those last happy years of her childhood? How would your son's growing into adulthood have been if you had not given him your continuing love and respect?'

The clock chimed four, singing of hope and new beginnings.

'What is that melody?' I asked, smiling.

'Whittington chime. You know the story of Dick Whittington, an apprentice running away from a cruel master? He heard that tune struck from the bell tower of the church at St Mary-le-Bow and they seemed to say to him, "Turn again, Whittington." So he did, and went on to become lord mayor of London.'

I smiled again and rose from my chair. 'Thank you so much!'

He offered to hug me and we stood quietly as I listened to the echoes of the tune in my head.

That's all I can remember from those sessions. I pondered his words and saw there was a pattern that I needed to decode. My personal story was part of a much bigger picture. The night after our first session, I woke from a dream in which I was writing in a book, but as I wrote, the words kept fading. It was like when I was a child and I'd tried writing with invisible ink. You dipped a pen with a nib into a cup of lemon juice and wrote a secret message on white paper. When it dried, you held it up to a lamp and you could read the words. Because you couldn't see the words as you wrote, you didn't know how the words would turn out, whether you'd got them right or there'd be mistakes.

My life was like that. I'd been writing what I thought was my life, my vision of how it would be – an equal love with a man, bringing up children together, giving them love and stability – but as I wrote the words, they faded, and each time I'd tried to create this vision, I'd failed.

The director was right. It was not my fault. The ink I'd been given to write with didn't work. The words weren't even true.

I reflected more on what had happened at work and in my dream. I'd been writing in a book that wasn't mine. I needed to write in my own book. I didn't want a career. I didn't want to become a psychotherapist. I didn't need to help other people whose lives were messy or broken. I needed to understand my own life and see why it had failed and how I could reset the pattern.

I wanted to write my story, to make sense of it. If I'd got that council job, I would have gone on filling services for clients and adjusting them as their needs or the budget changed. I was working ten hours a day including driving time. I was earning just enough to pay my bills and service my credit card debt. I had no savings, no assets and no way of getting ahead. What did it all matter anyway? Yes, I was helping people, but I was part of a system and what I could do for them was limited by the system.

The director of the Churchill Centre suggested I go back to uni and do a higher degree. 'You've clearly got the intelligence to do it. In the past, you were limited by your circumstances and by what the system had to offer. Things have opened up in higher education. You should be able to find a supervisor and a department that will support you to write and theorise your story.' He gave me the name of a couple of people to contact at Curtin University.

I made an appointment with a woman who was associate professor in Communication and Cultural Studies. I told her why I was there and gave her a resumé of my life story.

She looked at me over her half-rimmed glasses. 'Hmm, very interesting. It sounds like the bourgeois family.'

What the fuck is the bourgeois family?

She wrote some names and titles on a piece of paper and handed them to me. 'Have a look at these. You can use the library without being enrolled, but you won't be able to borrow books until you are. Come back and see me next week, and if you're happy to go ahead with me supervising you, we can get started.'

I spent several days in the library reading some of the texts she had listed. I learned that the position of a woman in the bourgeois family is impossible. A woman is subject to the man's desires and to his power. The condition of monogamy upon which marriage is constructed creates repression and boredom and suppresses desire, at least for the woman. Traditionally, a man is much freer to seek fulfilment outside the marriage than a woman. Desire is constructed as masculine and active, and if a woman seeks her object of desire outside the marriage, she becomes a fallen woman without status or value. A man more easily holds onto his status, even if he deserts his wife for another woman.

I saw this pattern in my mother's marriage and my own. I could see that, although this template of marriage had reached its heyday in the 1950s and family life was entering a more transitional state, many women were still trapped in those patterns that are stamped into the unconscious life of the individual and the family.

The Whittington chimes stayed with me in those years. As I studied feminist theories of women's subjectivity and desire and the patriarchal construction of childhood and parenthood and marriage and reflected on my parents' and grandparents' lives and my marriages, I experienced a continuing epiphany. That chime and the director's words were like a polished round stone thrown into the waters of a still lake, causing ripples to flow out from the centre and the energy of my life to shift into another register.

I became a full-time student at Curtin, and enrolled in a Master of Creative Arts degree. I didn't have a scholarship because it had been so long since my first degree, so I continued to work part-time as a carer. At the end of the first year, I'd completed two units of study in research methods and creative writing, but I was no closer to writing my story.

I sat in my theory supervisor's office and told her I needed to start writing my story. 'Is there someone who can supervise me?'

'I'll send you to the head of department. He writes biography and has supervised several creative students. Write a short piece for him, about a thousand words, and send it to him with a note.'

I knew the head was her life partner, and I wondered about whether the arrangement would work. I'd gone to a couple of seminars he'd given and I wasn't confident he could help me. Despite my misgivings, I wrote a scene from my life and sent it to him.

He handed my piece back to me and said, 'You need a structure. You need to plan how you are going to write this. Will you write it chronologically or will you construct it some other way?'

He went on about different ways of structuring life stories. Then, he looked at my few pages again and said, 'Why are you writing this? What do you have to tell the world that people don't already know?'

I stared back at him, lost for words. I'd told him at the beginning about the bourgeois family and how the patterns of my life fitted that frame. Didn't that tell him how my story, though it followed a pattern, was important, unique, needed to be told? Wasn't that enough?

I went back to my supervisor and told her I didn't want him to supervise me. I wanted a woman who understood why I was writing my story.

Sixteen

My creative supervisor was a lecturer in her thirties who was doing her PhD, which involved writing a novel. She was lovely, very empathic, and not at all condescending. I felt equal with her and understood. She had to go to Queensland for six months, to consult with her external supervisor at Queensland University.

It was 1999 and I didn't have the internet, so I would send her what I'd written and after a long pause she would return it to me with pencil writing in the margins. Many of the comments were variations on 'Cut back!' 'We don't need to know this.' 'Let the reader imagine.' 'Let the reader read between the lines here.'

When I felt I'd finished the story, I sent her the whole manuscript.

A couple of weeks later, she rang me. She said positive things about it, then asked me to make some notes. 'I want you to put page breaks at the end of each chapter. Then print it out. Think of your story as having three acts. Each act is part of the curve the story takes, building to a climax from an initiating conflict, then reaching a resolution. Within each act, there are scenes. Take the chapters and shuffle them, then pick out the ones that fit each act and arrange them in sequence. Then see if you need to do any rewriting so they fit together seamlessly.'

I cried for two hours after that. I'd written it chronologically, and at the time that seemed enough. Now I could see it was raw, it needed more shape. The ingredients were there but I had to find the pattern that would hold them in the best order.

Eventually, I felt satisfied with it, and she said she was too. I wanted to submit my work. The problem was my theory supervisor. She wrote all over my pages in red biro, rearranging and rewriting my sentences.

One morning I was getting ready to attend a seminar in the afternoon, where we were to present some of our work to a panel of staff. I was with a writing buddy, Sally, in the photocopy room.

The photocopier whirs and clicks. My head feels strange, tight around the temples, and the room is unbearably stuffy. The shapes of things are wobbly, and there is a bright white light at the edges of my vision.

'I think I'd better go and sit outside in the fresh air. I feel queer.'

Sally stops sorting her sheets of paper and turns to me. 'You do look pale. I'll come with you.'

We sit outside on a step in the shade.

'I think it might be an attack like the one I had the other night. I'm scared I might pass out. I think I should go to the toilet. Last time it happened I needed to…'

'Come on, I'll help you.'

Sally takes my arm, but I have a strange feeling that it's not my body that she's touching.

The light is weird, white and piercingly bright, like millions of stars joined together, and I cannot see the building in front of me.

I am lying on the floor. Someone is cradling my head. Sally is beside me, holding my hand. I cannot see her, but I know it is her, I can smell the perfume she always wears. Have I wet my pants? God, I hope not. I feel wet all over, but I think that is sweat.

'Call the ambulance!' A male voice behind me.

I cannot stop shaking, my heart thumps so fast I am afraid it will burst. I cannot get enough air.

'It's OK.' Sally's voice, low and urgent. 'I'm here. You'll be OK. We're getting the ambulance to take you to the clinic.'

You are in an alien world where there is only light, no shadow. It slices your head open, lays out all the circuits of your brain, exposes your secrets. You wish you could turn the light off. Even when you close your eyes, you can see it.

'Who's that holding my head?'

'Bruce. It's OK. We're getting a pillow. Where's that bloody ambulance?'

Bruce! Someone in the department with the name Bruce. No idea of the body attached to the voice. I wish I could see his face.

You are hot – unbearably hot; you would like to rip off your clothes. If you could find the words, you would curse those black satin trousers. You feel like a roasted chook wrapped in foil, waiting for the knife to slice open your steaming flesh.

'Where am I?'

'Near the lifts, on the way to the toilet,' Sally says. 'You passed out before we got there.'

It is not like the false sleep of anaesthesia, from which you wake muffled and dazed by drugs. It is a hole in your life, in your memory. Before is a blank. Now, though you are the centre of attention, you feel nothing but bewilderment and terror.

'Christ, that ambulance is taking its time.' Bruce's voice again. 'What the hell are they doing?'

Someone places a pillow under my head, and he withdraws his hands. I cannot stop shivering.

Though you are still sweating, steaming hot, you are also cold, an Arctic cold that is coming from inside, deeper than the heat. It feels like global warming speeded up, a sun that is out of control melting icebergs ocean-deep. This light has no soft tones. It is just white, absolute white, and it melts the world it once warmed.

Voices fade in and out.

'The ambulance can't get through. They have to move the bollards.'

'What a bloody shambles!' Sally's voice. 'I must remember not to get sick when I'm in here!'

'Find a blanket from somewhere. She's shivering.'

I fight for breath. Voices murmur.

You still cannot see properly. But instead of blinding white light, everything is dark. Shapes appear and disappear, shadows waver and reform, only to fade again.

'Can you climb onto this trolley?' An unfamiliar female voice.

I try to sit up, but my body is so weak and heavy, it will not move. My head flops back onto the pillow.

'You'll have to lift her. Can't you see she's helpless?' Sally's voice is sharp with exasperation and anxiety.

I am carried out. I shut my eyes against the bright light and can only sense the trolley being lifted and pushed into the back of a van. Sally climbs in beside me.

'Sally…you go to the seminar…you'll miss it.'

'Don't be silly. I'm coming with you.'

She was with me before this started. I remember now. We were in the photocopying room, talking about our theses.

So that's how I ended up in this bumpy van, flat out on a narrow trolley. I concentrate on my breathing, trying to slow it down.

At the clinic, they do an ECG, and explain that there are some irregularities, so I will need to go to the emergency department at the hospital to have some more tests.

Armed with a letter from the emergency registrar on duty, I go to see my GP.

She puts the letter down and takes off her glasses. 'Has there been much stress in your life recently?'

'Well…in a way. I'm doing my Masters at uni and…'

'What subject?'

'Master of Creative Arts. I'm writing a novel and a thesis.'

'What's it about?'

'My life. My childhood and my first marriage, which ended disastrously.'

She nods, as if to say, go on.

'I lost my children. My husband took them to America, and it was nearly two years before I saw them again.'

'Did you get them back?'

'Not when they were children. After I got access to them, I saw them once a year, till they came to Melbourne to live, and then I saw them twice a year. But my youngest came to live with me when she turned fourteen.'

I start to cry. I cannot help it. Twenty-seven years later and I still cannot talk about it without crying.

She pushes a box of tissues towards me. What did they do before tissues were invented? Did they offer their hankies, pressed and clean, or part-used?

I take a deep breath and blow my nose. 'I'm sorry. I guess I've never got over it. That's why I'm writing my life. I just want to…make sense of it.'

'Is it helping?'

'Yes. But there's a lot of stress in doing it. My theory editor writes all over my drafts in red ink. I thought I'd be finished the theory part by now – I've been on it long enough – but she wants me to do yet another rewrite. And last month, my creative supervisor asked me to rearrange the novel, mix up the different stages of the story, instead of having it sequential. I cried for two hours after I put the phone down.' I pause, and swallow. My throat feels tight and dry. 'Can I get a glass of water?'

She fills a paper cup from the water cooler near the door and hands it to me. 'What was it about mixing it all up that upset you?'

'I don't know. It felt like losing my children all over again.'

'Why? Is it like you've lost control of the story and it's not your story any more?'

I take another gulp of water. 'No, not really. I know it's something I have to go through, if I want to tell my story. But sometimes I wish I could just close the book and let it lie.'

'What made you start writing it?'

'Well… I started years ago, when Sophia, my eldest daughter begged me to. She said that I'm the one who inspired her to write, and I wasn't using my gift. She felt I needed to tell my story. So I started scribbling in an old exercise book at night when I went to bed, but I didn't get further than a few fragments.'

I tell her the story of how I went back to uni after I decided I needed to tell my story and make sense of it.

'Well...' She sits back in her chair and stares at the wall for a moment, as if she's looking for the right words. 'Clearly it's very stressful – not only reliving your story, but letting other people have a say in how you tell it. Yet I imagine it's therapeutic too.' She takes up the letter from the registrar and scans it again. 'The doctors in casualty found no physical cause for your attack. Does it make sense to you that it was a panic attack?'

'I don't know. I felt like I was dying. But it wasn't the first time. It happened once before when I was watching TV. I was feeling quite relaxed at the time, eating a roast lamb dinner. I felt as though I wanted to go to the toilet then too, and my vision went funny. I collapsed halfway to the toilet, but I didn't pass out. I called my son, and he came and helped me first to the toilet and then into bed. I was shaking and shivering. My son called the locum doctor. He took my blood pressure, pulse and temperature, and said it was a fast virus. It took me hours to warm up. This last time, I just got too hot.'

The doctor looks unconvinced.

'I was in the photocopying room. It gets really stuffy in there.'

'OK, but the way the body works, you don't need to be feeling anxious when the attack happens. There's an overload of stress that builds up over time. Whatever triggers the attack might have happened some time before, and you think you've dealt with it. But the stress stays in the body and has to be discharged somehow.'

'But...I always thought panic attacks happen when you're feeling anxious – like women panicking in supermarkets or busy public places. And I don't feel anxious at the time – not until after the attack starts. That's when I start to panic, because I feel as though I'm dying.'

'I know, but regardless of what you're aware of, you must have a very high base level of anxiety for this to happen. All those symptoms you get are from a sudden discharge of stress hormones.'

I walk out of her office with a prescription for an antidepressant to reduce my anxiety. She says there won't be any side effects once I'm used to it. To my relief, she doesn't recommend counselling. I've had enough of baring my soul. This time I want to work through it myself. But I cannot afford to have more attacks. What if it happens while I'm driving a car? Or in a public place where no one knows me? I just want to get my thesis finished and move on.

A couple of weeks after my visit to the GP, Sophia suggests I stay at their time share unit at Busselton for a couple of days. They're packing to move to their new house, and she wants me to wait there for her with her younger son, Stevie, and her husband and older boy will join us the next day. She says she needs twenty-four hours to get the last of the packing done without having to worry about Stevie. I hesitate, because I'm concerned I might have another attack, but I haven't had one for about two weeks, and I think by now the antidepressant must be working. So I say yes.

Stevie sits in the safety seat behind me, and we sing nursery rhymes together until my voice starts to crack. He gets a bit restless, so we stop for a while at a lay-by, and I take him on a short ramble through the bush looking for wildflowers. After biscuits and milk for him, and coffee from the thermos for me, we get going. He drops off to sleep, and I have a peaceful hour.

Everything feels fine until an old Datsun swerves out of the inside lane and cuts in front of me to take a right turn. I slam on the brakes. No time to check the rear-vision mirror. I hear an echoing squeal of brakes behind me. The lights turn red but the driver of the Datsun, a young male, keeps going.

I wind down the window, stick my head out and scream, 'Fucking idiot!' I look in the mirror. Stevie is still sleeping, chin on chest, beads of sweat on his forehead.

Deep breaths, I tell myself. My head feels tight and my heart is pounding. The lights turn green, and I continue, moving into the left lane, dropping my speed to eighty ks. I push a tape – Mozart's piano concertos – into the player and check the mirror again. Stevie sleeps on. I breathe down into my stomach and out very slowly.

We arrive as the sun is setting. After unloading the car, I take Stevie down to the beach. He runs, chasing seagulls, and I follow his winding path, little footprints in the wet sand.

It's three a.m. I've woken up with a start, feeling strange. It's starting again. I scramble out of bed to get to the toilet before it's too late.

I wake up on the bedroom carpet, shivering and shaking. I'm halfway across the room, between the bed and the bathroom. I've shat myself. I lie for what seems like an hour, trying to breathe, my heart pounding. At last, I can get up and struggle to the shower. I stand under the hot water, trying to warm up. After I've dried myself and changed my nightie, I clean the carpet and crawl back into bed. I'm so cold I can't get back to sleep. I just lie there watching the hours tick by, until Stevie calls me from his room after sunrise.

The rest of the day is hard to get through. My head feels strange after these attacks, and I feel weak and tired. I try to explain to Stevie that I'm not well, but he just looks at me as if I'm weird. At last, the rest of the family arrive.

Sophia suggests I phone Maggie, a psychologist who has experience working with people who suffer from panic attacks. I can't afford to go and see her professionally, but Sophia says she won't mind me ringing for a chat.

Maggie tells me she has treated a lot of people who have had attacks like mine, though she hasn't known many who have actually lost consciousness. She says she teaches them to relax when they feel the first symptoms, to flow toward the fear, rather than away from it. She says the more you resist and try to pull back from what's happening, the more stress you create in yourself, the worse the experience will be. Easier said than done. But I will try.

I'm sitting at my computer, retyping the last chapter of my novel. I hope this is the last draft. I'll send it off tomorrow, and if I get it back within the month, I'll be able to submit my thesis this year. My theory supervisor has at last agreed that the exegesis is ready to be examined.

My head begins to throb, and my temples tighten. Oh shit! Not again. I jump up from the chair and move towards the toilet. Hope I make it.

I'm lying face down. A wet nose pushes into my cheek. A doggy smell. Snuffles. I'm on the kitchen floor. My heart is pounding and I can't get my breath. I think I'll die this time. Alone.

You can get through this. Slow your breath. Feel the cold linoleum against your cheek. You won't die.

No idea how long I've been here. Feels like an hour. I can breathe deeper now. Cold. I feel so cold. And I have to get to the toilet. I pull myself up onto my hands and knees, and crawl down the step, into the laundry, and hoist myself up onto the toilet. Relieved, I stand, holding onto the wall, and walk slowly to my bedroom. I collapse on the bed and pull the doona over me. I curl up, hugging myself. My feet are freezing.

You didn't die. Your son will come home in a while and look after you, and tomorrow you will finish your novel and post it off.

I'm helping Sophia unpack her kitchen stuff in their new house.

'Have you had any more panic attacks, Mum?'

'Just that one on the kitchen floor I told you about. That was the worst. I really felt I would die. But somehow, facing it on my own, I felt stronger afterwards.'

'Did you try what Maggie suggested?'

'I don't think so. It happened so suddenly.' As we speak, my temples start to feel tight, and the light shifts and whitens. 'Oh no, I think it's starting again.'

'Sit down, Mum. Try and relax.' She helps me into the living room.

I sink onto the soft couch and take some deep breaths. I hear Maggie's voice.

'Flow towards the fear, not away from it.'

I imagine myself floating towards the white light, allowing it to enfold me. After a few minutes, my breath quietens, and my heart slows down. But I am cold. So I go to the bedroom and crawl under the doona. After a while, I feel almost normal again.

Ready for some more unpacking.

Seventeen

What did it mean, that part of my life? Looking back, it seems such a muddle. So much unhappiness, so many moves of house. From when I left the children with Robert till now, a rough count comes up at thirty-five. Twenty of those were in Western Australia. Four separations from Michael, two marriages and two divorces with him. Fifteen years between the second divorce and our final reunion. Two Pilbara towns, two wheatbelt towns. In none of those was I happy. When we finally became lovers again, we were both old. I was sixty-six, he was seventy-five. I thought we had found the love we both sought, that we were able to meet equally and with mutual desire. But our hearts were unequal. He wanted a lover and a good companion. I wanted to share my life with him. He didn't want to be responsible for me or for me to be responsible for him.

I think I realised this some time before we actually separated again. We went to Cervantes, a fishing town on the coast north of Perth, for a weekend. I hoped that this would give us space to see if we could live together.

Seaweed Dreams

I wade through the green jelly water. It's wobbly, as if someone didn't put in enough gelatine. It sways and swells over white angel cake sand. The shallow shelf stretches far out, and the water pales to a lighter shade of green, then darkens. I turn round before I get to the darker part, afraid of sharks. If one comes, will I see it in time? Will I make it back to shore? Will he see or hear in time to help me if I am attacked?

I'm bored with safe, shallow water, but I'm afraid of the deep.

He launches himself backwards in the shallower water, a skinny white seal, letting the water lap over his stiff, aching arms and legs. He's more at home in the water than I am. But he's cautious about going out too far because his legs are weak.

'They're far enough away not to take offence,' he'd said as he stripped off.

The group of adults, children and dogs are splashing in the shallows further along the long thin curve of white sand. If they notice his nakedness, they may see him as just an eccentric old man taking a health cure. If this were a Perth beach, he wouldn't get away with it. We've come here looking for informality and freedom to do as we like. Suburbia lurks in the ordered streets of the crayfishing town. Where once there were shacks and simple cottages, now there are kit homes interspersed with solid brick residences and the occasional crayfisher's mansion. But here, on the beach beyond the town limits, we are nomads escaping from the great sprawl of the city and the long street of respectable houses that is this town. Escaping from our escape.

I breaststroke towards him, helped by the gentle swell of waves. This is perfect. I hate swimming out of my depth, in water where I can't see the bottom. I can't bear putting my head under water, ever since I nearly drowned as a child.

His penis and balls sway as he floats. Soft, plump sea creatures against his white thighs and groin fuzzed with fine dark hair like seaweed strands. He turns his lanky body and moves languidly through the wobbly green jelly water. He lets the water carry him, swelling and ebbing in a gentle rhythm.

I love him more than ever. More than I did when he and I were young, when he wanted me and I left him. I feared love then.

The wet sand is edged by a shelf of dry powdery sand, tossed with bundles of seaweed. A tangle of broad flat olive-brown lasagne, curly-edged bronze pappardelle, messes of fine russet capella d'angelo, laced with strings of tiny acid-green beads.

Back at the house, the day is long and hot. I am lethargic. He sleeps, curled on his side, his silver hair and brown face exotic against royal purple bed linen. A beached Neptune. And I, his consort, once Medusa to his Poseidon; now, we are older and more at home with fresh water than with the unruly depths of the sea. I lie down beside him, not because I'm tired, but for the closeness of his body. I twist and turn, settling on my back, waiting for thoughts of everyday life to fade. I hardly ever sleep during the day, but if I relax enough, a conversation begins in my head. Voices speak of other lives, other selves.

After lunch, I prepare a lamb shank casserole for dinner: shanks seared in olive oil, bedded on garlic, celery and root vegetables, splashed with red wine, fish sauce and balsamic vinegar and seasoned with mustard, marjoram and black pepper. I add ruby-red whole tomatoes in thick juice to sweeten the sauce, and barley to give a nutty texture.

He washes up two days' dishes, and we laugh together at the *Goon Show* on CD. Crazy nomadic humour, that makes fun of the conventions of English class society. We both lived there, separately, at the same time, so we share a loving nostalgic view of it, peppered with down-under mockery of their stuffier ways. It brings us close again. The waves sway and swell, ebb and flow, and we float with them.

After dinner, we watch a documentary about a white man who lives for a time with a central African tribe of forest people. He is to be initiated, a gruelling process of eating bark that contains a powerful hallucinogen. He is apprehensive because he knows the drug will activate sites in the brain that hold memories of past relationships, in particular ones in which he has behaved without kindness or concern for the other person. The men of the tribe are not sure what dose to give him, as they have not initiated a white man before. He signs a paper absolving them of responsibility if it should go amiss.

He vomits in spasms until he is possessed by visions. The film doesn't disclose the visions he has, for they are secret men's business, but he says that he has visited some painful and guilty memories, made even more uncomfortable by the fact that he experienced how it felt to be the person he had wronged. As he leaves the village, he tells how his life has been changed by the love shown him there, by reliving his past and realising his lack of care for others. He desires reconciliation with those he has wronged.

We sit out on the balcony, sipping the last glass of wine for the day; we are cooled by a light wind from the sea. The intense heat of the day has gone, and the darkening sky is beaded with mackerel clouds.

We talk of the man's initiation. I compare it with western psychoanalysis. But the depth of the experience, the intensity and specificity of it seem much more powerful.

'What I found fascinating was that he was able to relive the past with hallucinatory intensity, not just remember and talk about it.'

'He was very brave,' Michael says.

'Would you do it?'

'No, I don't think so. I'd be afraid of taking the wrong dose, of losing control…'

I wonder – if he could do it, if he could relive some times in our relationship, see it from my point of view, would it change the present? Would it deepen his understanding of me and perhaps of his own nature if he could really enter into my feelings and not just guess at them? How much does he know of my inner thoughts and feelings? Can he ever know how it is or was to be me?

He is an island I trawl around, making a landing sometimes, camping for a while, meeting his body and mind, joining, then separating.

I remind myself that the same applies to me. I think of the times I have rejected him, withheld my love, left him, taking our son with me. It's much easier to see things from my point of view than from his.

I don't say any of this.

We can't relive those times. But they keep coming back, and right now I wish that we could eat or drink something that would let us relive the past, so that we could understand it better from each other's point of view, then let go of it. It's because we can never go there again that it haunts us. How would it be if we could go back, if we could choose differently?

Perhaps it would be so painful it would destroy us. We wouldn't be able to measure the dose of remembering, we would be sucked into the other's experience, living it otherwise, unable to step back and say, 'It's not me.' But I am him, he is me. We have hurt each other, we can't change that. Perhaps, without the hallucinogenic bark, we can only live in the present. We hurt ourselves, now we can be happy again. We can have one more birth.

There is no cause and effect. There is only now.

We don't speak. He sits for a while, then gets up from his chair and goes downstairs. I stay, finishing my wine. I make a desultory effort to finish the crossword and word puzzle. I wonder if he is upset about something, or just tired. His moods aren't sharp, but he has times when he is remote and shut off. He's always been like it. He is much more passionate than me, but he switches on and off. I used to take it personally; I felt it was me he was rejecting. Now I know it's a protective thing; he is a sea creature that floats with the tide, that pulses and opens to the caress of shallow water suffused by sunlight, retreats with the dark and the deepening tide, closes, then opens again.

In bed, after I've showered and turned off the main light, he puts down his book and reaches for me.

We begin to kiss, and suddenly, I am overtaken by a wild playfulness. Is it him, or is it me, growling like a jungle creature? I echo him, he echoes me in a chorus of animal calls. I am possessed as I roll on top of him, and he enters me at once. Mimicry gives way to screams of ecstatic surrender as he thrusts, again and again and again. We roll over. A moment of quiet, then he begins again. Another crescendo. Can that be me, caterwauling?

We lie still for a few moments, then stir, and we are animal again. He shouts and groans like one dying in agony.

Beyond the shallows, the water is deep and dark, and I reach down with my toes and touch a soft, spongy reef, ancient rocks covered with a thick quilting of seaweed, inhabited by many tiny creatures of the sea. My toes curl, my body softens and relaxes, sways and drifts with the swell of the waves.

Now, we drift together.

A year after our seaweed dreams, we sit facing each other in his living room. He has asked me to move in with him. I say, 'Well, I need a little time to think about it. It's a big commitment to make, and I would have to give up most of my furniture…it wouldn't fit in here. And I'd need a separate bedroom. I love going to bed with you, but I can't spend the night with you because you snore and I'm a light sleeper.'

When he drifts off to sleep – sleep comes easily for him – he puffs his lips and blows warm air into my neck. Then his legs twitch, and as he falls deeper, walrus snores erupt.

'I can set up the spare room for you. And I'm sure we could fit your favourite pieces of furniture in.'

'Well, there's another thing. You're nine years older than me, and it may be that you will die before me. In that case, I'd have no place of my own and I'd have to find somewhere to rent.'

I know that he has willed his estate to his three children, including the house.

'So, would it be possible for you to put a clause in your will saying that I could stay in the house until I find somewhere suitable to live… say for a maximum of six months? So I wouldn't have to move out straight away?'

He looks at me and takes another sip of whisky. 'Well, perhaps. I'd need to speak to my kids about that.'

I know there is something more I need to make clear. 'The other thing is, Michael, you know, if you need help to live independently… I don't need to be your carer. We could get help. There are plenty of services to help people go on living in their own homes.'

He told me he doesn't want me to be his carer. He has a horror of losing his independence. But he has health issues – chronic back pain, hearing loss, and other side effects of ageing.

He drains his whisky and looks at me, his eyes veiled. 'Aahh, I don't know. I'll have to think about it.'

A week later, I ask him if he's made a decision.

'Umm, I guess so.' He blinks and looks down at his feet.

'What?' I can feel what is coming.

He meets my eyes then looks away. 'I can't do it.'

'What is it you can't do?'

'I don't know… I just don't feel able to share everyday life with you. I… I don't want to feel responsible for anyone else.'

'You don't need to. I'm responsible for myself. Is it because I asked you to put a clause in your will?'

'Well…' He hesitates. 'Yes. I can't do that.'

'Why not?'

He stands up and walks across to the kitchen to put the jug on. 'Coffee?'

'No thanks.'

He has a habit of drinking black coffee before he goes to bed, even sipping it in bed sometimes. I never understand how he can do it and then go straight to sleep.

'Why can't you do it?'

He turns to face me. 'I don't trust you. I think if your back is up against the wall, you might take something from my kids that's not yours.'

I stare at him. All those years, all the times we separated, I'd agreed to his terms, except the last time, when I left him in that wheatbelt town where he had the pharmacy and insisted we have a formal separation agreement and he pay an allowance for Sebastian until he was eighteen and a year's wages in recognition of the work I'd done in the pharmacy. I'd stayed in Western Australia for a third of my life because of him. I'd been there thirty years and most of that time I'd wanted to return to Sydney. But I didn't want to take his son away, to do to him what Robert had done to me.

I turn and pick up my bag. 'I'll go now, Michael.' I shake my head to push the tears away. 'You don't know me.'

I moved down from the hills to be near him two years ago, so he wouldn't have to drive all that way to see me. I took a flat in a beach suburb near him. I arranged my life around him, holding onto the dream we could be together and give each other love and companionship for as long as life allowed. I made a mistake – again. It has never worked between us; it never will.

Eighteen

It's 2008 and I'm in the final stages of my PhD, continuing my inquiry into women's desire and how it is constructed in a patriarchal world, how it can be unfolded and refolded. I've enjoyed this journey, moving from Foucault and Freud to post-structural philosophy and a couple of radical French theorists. From the closed room that Freud and Foucault left me in, where children's polymorphic desires are repressed and incestuous, I have entered a universe where creativity can be freed from the chains of culture and orthodox morality. Where we can move from the restrictions of the world we have inherited and the fictions of selfhood and habit to form new connections and transformations.

My studies are interrupted by the eruption of old patterns, created in my children's childhood by the choices their father and I made. My beloved middle daughter, Caitlin, who rebelled against her father's and stepmother's tyranny, is going through another crisis. Her life in a coastal town in south-west Western Australia is falling apart. Her love marriage is broken and she is gripped again by addiction, this time, to alcohol.

I have come down to stay with her and her three boys for a while, to help her to recover her balance and look after her children. I couldn't help her when she was a child, locked into an abusive family. I failed her then. I won't fail her now.

The two younger boys are asleep, Sol is reading. It's been a long day. I tuck myself into bed, drawing the doona up around my chin; it's a cold spring night, the wind whistles through the gaps in the boards. I read for a while, then turn the light out. Tomorrow morning early, Caitlin has an appointment with her GP, and I must make sure I get her there, so her doctor is aware of how bad things are.

I wake at two thirty and get up for a pee. On the way back, I step into Caitlin's room to see if she is OK. There's just enough light from the open door to the hallway to show me her bed is empty. Where can she be? I check that both cars are still there, parked in the driveway. I hid the keys last night when we got home, after I'd poured the rest of her gin out of the water bottle onto the grass and put her to bed. My heart is thumping fast.

It's a cold night. She surely can't have walked into town. Perhaps she's lying unconscious somewhere. I check all round the house, under the house, calling her name, but not too loud, in case I wake the children; I open the door of the caravan and peer in.

It's empty. Back in the house, I find her purse on the desk, and go through it. There's no money but her bankcard is still there. I dial the police and get through to the nearest regional centre. The local police station isn't manned at night. The policeman I speak to takes her details but says they can't do anything till morning. He asks me to let them know if I find her.

I'd better ring Simon, her ex. I try his mobile number, and he answers. I say I think she may have walked into town last night after I'd gone to bed, to get more alcohol. He says he will drive around and look for her. I get my doona and sit outside on the veranda, waiting. An hour goes past. I see his old car driving past slowly, rattling and wheezing. It cruises down to the end of the street, then turns and goes back. At last, he drives up and tells me he has looked in all the likely places and can't see her. I tell him I'll phone him if she turns up.

After he's gone, I go back to bed, closing my burning eyes. What if we find her body in the morning? What if she has overdosed? How will I tell the children? I picture them at her funeral, white faced and silent.

In this long night, I review all the steps that have brought us to this point. Her childhood before I left – the little girl with the broad face and bright blue eyes, the head that seemed too big for her body, the

floss of red-gold curls and radiant smile. Then, all the painful partings, watching her and her sisters trail across the tarmac to the plane in the wake of the air hostess, turning to wave to me before they climbed the stairs. The time she was eleven years old, when she told me she didn't want to go back to Melbourne, and that her stepmother hit and abused her and Penelope. She hinted at problems with her stepbrother, too.

My lawyer and my brother advised me that I must send her back, as her father had custody, and go through a legal process and testify against her family. Unless there was evidence of serious ill treatment, it was unlikely a judge would award me custody.

I had no choice. What could I do, from three thousand miles away?

I continued to see them twice a year, and Caitlin became more withdrawn and sullen. Once, after she had gone home, I found an opened packet in the rubbish bin; it contained a needle for a syringe. She had visited me at the hospital where I worked in the psychiatric outpatients' unit. I phoned her and told her what I'd found. She said she'd just been curious, that she hadn't used the needle. I told her she could come and live with me if she wanted to, that I would do whatever it took to bring her over. She said she was all right. That was when she had said she knew she would be a better person if she lived with me, but she didn't want to leave her dad and her sisters.

When she was seventeen, she went to England. She had been living there for a couple of years when I learned that she was a street prostitute and a heroin addict.

Again, I was powerless to help. What saved her was an arrest for dealing and possession, and her father's intervention through a lawyer, who got her released on a bond, on condition she returned to Perth to live with me, as she requested.

When she arrived in Perth, she was on a reducing dose of methadone, which she had obtained illegally. I took her to my GP, who prescribed codeine over a few days to see her through withdrawals, and she admitted herself to a rehabilitation clinic.

Her life since then seemed to be happy and successful, with rehab, training in youth work and university studies, falling in love and starting a family, living in a supportive, creative community in the south-west. But her relationship has fallen apart and her business has been staggering for the last couple of years. Her descent into alcoholism took us all by surprise. She says she has been drinking heavily for years, but I didn't know and nor did her sisters.

I'd been on several rescue missions in the last six months, supporting her after brief hospital admissions to detox. The last time, she had spent two weeks at a Buddhist retreat, where she did well. She had come home with my support, but collapsed again when I drove to Perth overnight to get some things I needed for a longer stay. The few days since then, she had been on a bender with brief sober patches in the mornings.

I toss and turn, counting the hours as the clock ticks beside my bed. It's getting light; I'd better get up and see if she's come home. A voice startles me; it's Simon.

'Sorry – she's back. I just checked. She's on her bed. She says she's been walking round for a few hours.' He stands in the doorway, running his fingers through his hair, staring at the floor. His hair is wild, his eyes red.

As he drives off, I walk into her room. She lies on the bed, in her tatty old tracksuit pants and windcheater, her hair tousled, bits of grass stuck in it. Her eyes are shut. I touch her shoulder.

'Caitlin – where have you been?'

'Walking,' she mutters.

I pull the doona up around her chin and leave her to sleep. Soon the children will be waking. I'll phone her sister and ask her to take them to school so I can take Caitlin to the doctor.

The long night is over, and I'll never know where she's been, what happened; she probably doesn't know herself. At least she came back.

The search for help between that night and now has been a difficult journey.

Caitlin was admitted to the local hospital for a couple of nights, and although we had an emergency admission to a detox unit in Perth arranged, it fell through because I took her home from hospital to pack her things and say goodbye to her children. When we phoned the detox unit to say we would be a little late, they said that an emergency admission meant a hospital-to-hospital transfer. Because I had taken her home first, they couldn't accept her. I hadn't been informed of the rule.

I tried to contact her doctor, but it was her day off. I tried to speak to her partner in the medical practice, and was told he couldn't speak to me, and I should take her to the nearest regional hospital. In the end, we drove to Perth (a six-hour drive) and went to the emergency centre of the central hospital, where she was eventually seen by a doctor and given a few Valium tablets to tide her over.

We were told the best option was for her to detox in the community. I took her home. We faced a holiday weekend before we could go to the detox centre and try to get her admitted. Over the next three days, she managed to get alcohol and drink secretly, until, on the third evening, I found her unconscious on her bed. I got an ambulance to take her to hospital, and they arranged her admission to the detox unit next morning.

After false starts and denial, she accepted that she was an alcoholic and travelled to Queensland with Sophia. She was in a Buddhist retreat for a couple of weeks with Sophia, and was now staying with Penelope and her family in the Gold Coast hinterland.

I helped Sophia look after the younger boys while Caitlin was trying to decide what to do – whether to return or make a life for herself in Queensland. She had intended to return to the boys, but realised that if she did, she would surely break down again, such was the toxic state of her relationship with the boys' father and the aftershock of her breakdown in the close-knit community. She phoned me to tell me and asked me to let them know.

I took a glass of wine and sat outside with them on the seat near the front door, where they were staying with Sophia and family. 'Caitlin has asked me to tell you that she can't come back. She's going to stay with Penelope and find a house she can rent, where you can visit her.' There was no way of putting this but bluntly. I tried to soften it. 'She wants you to know that she is doing this so she can stay healthy and strong and make a home for you. She knows that if she comes back here, the things that happened before are likely to happen again.'

Sol, the eldest, was not with us; he was staying with his father and his new partner. Max, the middle boy, is very close to Caitlin. He looked shocked when I told him.

Liam, the youngest, looked at me and said, 'I understand. Cos that's what I would do.' I hugged them both and marvelled at the wisdom of this seven-year-old.

Caitlin is doing well with Penelope. The experience of abandonment and abuse in childhood forged very strong bonds between the three sisters. I am relieved that Sophia was able to go with her and support her. We didn't feel safe to let her go on her own, and I was exhausted and starting to panic about finishing my thesis. I am content that she is staying with Penelope in a happy, healthy, drug- and alcohol-free environment, with access to community support.

I am picking up the pieces of my life, thankful that at last she has been able to accept help. Last night, I went to an Italian restaurant with my son, his wife and father. While we sat waiting for the others to arrive, a young man left the table behind us with his girlfriend. He paused beside my chair, rubbed me gently on the back and told me he hoped my cough would get better. He suggested I boil lemon peel in water and drink the water with honey. His touch was gentle and loving; I was moved by the random act of kindness and love from a complete stranger, his innocence and openness in bridging the usual rigid gap between strangers.

I felt intensely aware of the loneliness of the last few weeks, the struggle to get help from those who were supposed to help, the difficulties and the silences, the covering up and the evasions, the refusal of her doctors to speak to me and include me in the treatment plan, the awful yawning gaps in the structure of society that can allow someone who needs and wants help to fall through and be lost, the waiting period of weeks between detox (if you can get in) and rehab in a safe place. How many people fall through the gaps? How many don't have anyone who is prepared or able to stand by them through the darkest time, to rescue them from themselves when they are helpless?

'I need to get her out of the family system,' her GP had said on the phone to the hospital staff when she was requesting a bed for her, after that long night when she went missing. I sat in the surgery next to Caitlin, who was hunched over, her head in her hands, her eyes half shut. What does she mean, I thought? Does she think I am part of the problem? I've been trying to save her, trying to protect her children, to stop her driving with them in the car when she can't see which side of the road she's driving on. Does she think I've caused this?

I suppose I did, all those years ago, when I left her and her sisters with a father who failed to protect her, and later the abusive woman he married with two children who bullied my daughters. Perhaps she is right. I am part of the problem.

But her sisters and I are also the only ones who have been able to go to the end of the road with her. Some of her friends have washed their hands of her, many have tried to help and failed, and I have stayed with her at some of the worst times and tried to keep her and her children safe. Perhaps it's poetic justice that it was just me and her in those dark days. I had to do what I'd been unable to do so many years before.

Nineteen

When I returned to university at fifty-nine, I found a community where I could share my story and find ways of theorising it, of understanding the underlying patterns that had repeated over and over in my life.

When I read Foucault and Freud, I came to understand that I had been born into the bourgeois family, constructed on the pattern of conjugal monogamy, with the man having superior power and agency and the woman assigned the roles of wife and mother. If she resisted or did not fulfil expectations, she could become the scarlet woman or a woman whose identity has been stripped, whose status is even more secondary than that of the wife.

In my PhD studies, I went beyond that victim archetype and began to see how I could free myself from the patterns that had been set for me. I saw, and see now, that we create the reality we live in. We can choose how we respond to others. We do not have to conform to their expectations. Our purpose in life is to be ourself.

This is the way I have learned to tell myself the story of my own life. Metaphors, myths and fairy stories help me to understand patterns and to see that the personal story I tell shares universal archetypes. I am Demeter, who lost her daughter Persephone and reclaimed her. I am Hecate, the temple goddess, who entered the dark world and faced the cruel sins of the underworld. I am Alice in Wonderland. When she falls down the rabbit burrow and seeks a way to get through the door into the world beyond, she eats the mushroom or drinks the magic drink but has little control over the results. She has to go through several metamorphoses until she can enter that world. When she does, of course, she is different from everyone else, and doesn't understand the things they say or the ways they behave.

Like Alice, I wanted to escape from the burrow of my first marriage into a place where I could be free to wander and to experience the wonders of adult life. I had no thought of leaving my children behind; I believed we were indissolubly linked. I broke the rules of marriage, as did my husband, but he did it in such a way that he was able to keep me and his children. I chose to reject him, and that choice branded me as the scarlet woman.

My children were stolen from me. I chose the wrong way to escape by taking a lover. But that was the language I'd grown up with: that a woman completes herself through the love of a man. And since I had lost the love of the man in my childhood, my father, I longed for that completion. I thought it would be a key to self-realisation and happiness. I didn't think through the consequences or realise how ruthless my husband would be if I stepped through that door.

The rest of my life, until I began to write my story, has been a series of experiences that didn't bring the freedom and fulfilment I hoped for.

All the men I loved, in one way or another, were unavailable. I thought love would bring happiness. I was happy, but only for brief passages. The best thing that my second marriage brought me was fulfilment through having another child, another chance to be a mother who could keep her child safe and help him grow into the person he wanted to be. And that, as well as being mother to my three daughters, has been the greatest gift of my life.

Motherhood to my daughters has often been painful, because of separation and witnessing their unhappiness and struggles. It has also been rewarding, because I have seen their courage and resilience and witnessed their growth into creative beings who share their gifts with others and help others to get in touch with their own inner gifts and express them.

When they were younger, our love, though never broken, was shadowed by our grief and regret and broken trust. There was no magic wand that could make that all vanish. It has been a gradual process, and for me, the healing has come through my service to them, especially through helping them to bring up their children.

When Sophia was a young mother with two little boys, aged six and less than two, she had to go back to work, as her husband was struggling to earn enough to support his family. She worked long hours and often did overtime. It was heart-breaking for her, who loved being a mother to her boys and had wanted to be a home mother to them while they were little.

I agreed to look after the boys during the day; their father was working from home. So I travelled for three-quarters of an hour to their home every weekday and did the household chores while I was looking after them. I was studying for my Masters degree then, so I had to balance that with housewifely duties, doing most of my reading and writing at nights and at the weekend.

The irony for me was that I was studying the construction of the bourgeois family, and there I was, back in it, in my late fifties and early sixties, cooking, washing up, hanging washing out, bringing it in, doing a little cleaning, taking the boys to preschool or school. The boys seemed to change their clothes every day, and so there were endless socks, underpants, shirts, trousers and more for laundry cycles. The bright side was my interaction with the boys, the stories, the TV shows they loved... *Thomas the Tank Engine, Bob the Builder.* Little Stevie was obsessed with Thomas and would spend hours laying out the wooden train set and moving the carriages and engines around, enacting the characters. I lived half in their world for about three years. I sometimes grumbled to myself about it, but I formed close bonds with both of them that have lasted through the years.

Twenty

After I graduated with my PhD, I worked for eighteen months at Curtin University. Towards the end of my second year there, I visited Penelope and her family in south-east Queensland. She had a boy aged seven whom I hadn't seen since he was three, and a girl aged three whom I had never seen. I had been too poor to travel over more often. Penelope's husband, Akira, was working as a tour guide at night, and she was teaching English five days a week at a Gold Coast university. Their household was like a revolving door; one would come home and the other would go to work, or he would have to get up after four hours' sleep and look after the children when she went to work before seven a.m.

Meanwhile, Caitlin had established a rented home for herself and her boys. Their father had died of cancer the year after he and Caitlin separated, and the two younger boys came to Queensland to be with their mother. Sol chose to stay in the country town in WA and finish high school, living with Sophia's family and with close family friends. Caitlin was running a market stall in Brisbane, selling cakes and slices that she baked at home. On market days, she left home early in the morning before the boys woke up and got home after they were in bed. She was managing it by dint of help from neighbours.

Both families needed my support. I went back to Western Australia knowing I would move over to be near them and support them and their families. It was a certainty, an inner knowing that I could not question. It wasn't entirely altruistic. Since I'd finished study and my work at Curtin, my life in Perth had seemed more peripheral. I wasn't sure what direction to take. I had wanted to leave Perth ever since I arrived there thirty-one years before. Now that I knew my relationship with Michael could not develop into anything more than an affectionate friendship, and that my son was living his own life, I felt freer to make my own way. I was beginning to support myself by editing PhD theses, so I wasn't tied to a place. Caitlin and Penelope both said they would love it if I lived closer to them, but they wanted me to do it for my own sake as much as for theirs. I couldn't separate the two.

It seemed to be a karmic turn in the wheel, a turning point as strong as the epiphany I had when I dropped thoughts of building a career and started to study and write my story. That turn had helped me to form an emotional and intellectual understanding of the patterns of my life and how they had been shaped by my childhood and my unconscious desires to change the template of my life, to shake free of the chains of the system I was born into. When study and university work were finished, I felt at a loose end, waiting for the next turn of the wheel to take place. My visit to Queensland had shown what that turn would be. I was needed by my two younger daughters, and Sophia and Sebastian no longer needed me as much as they had. And I needed to be of service as a mother and grandmother as well as to evolve my selfhood. It was an instant decision for me, without any shadow stage of uncertainty and doubt such as I had before I moved over to Perth.

Two months later, I put my car on the Indian Pacific, having hired a removalist to take my furniture across by road, and I travelled on the train to Sydney, then drove my car up to the Gold Coast.

It took me a few months to find the right house to rent in this country town a few miles inland from the coast in a fertile valley in northern New South Wales, near the Border Ranges. For the next two or three years, while working at home as an editor, I travelled over the mountain three or four mornings a week. I would go to Penelope's and get the children their breakfast, prepare their lunches, see them off to school or play group, and have a coffee with Akira when he woke up. On Caitlin's market day, I would go to her house in time to wake the boys, help them with breakfast and packed lunches, and take them to their separate schools. I would drive home over the mountain and do some editing. Then, in the afternoon, I would drive over the mountain again and pick them up from school, take them home, prepare dinner and eat it with them, and then drive home before Caitlin arrived back from the market. She would text me to let me know she was home, and I would let her know I was home safe.

In 2019, Akira became ill and was diagnosed with cancer. It was a late diagnosis, and the cancer was already well established. He chose not to have conventional treatment and went to Thailand to do a juice purge with meditation and other healing rituals.

The year of his dying was a very painful one for them. I stepped in to help as much as I could. When the diagnosis of terminal cancer was confirmed, Penny was able to get payment of his life insurance, which enabled her to pay off their mortgage and stay at home to nurse him.

Two families, broken apart by separation, both needing help and support. I am so grateful that I've been able to help them, and that earlier, I was able to support Sophia and her family. This has been a healing journey for us all. The dark gift of separation in their childhood has been met with the alchemy of love and shared burdens, and, like kintsugi, golden repair, has mended the broken pot of our shared lives with gold.

In kintsugi, lacquer is dusted or mixed with powdered gold, silver or platinum and the broken pieces are joined together again. Breakage or repair is part of the history of an object, rather than something to disguise. It is similar to the art of wabi-sabi, an embracing of the flawed or imperfect. The repair is literally illuminated and the value of the object increases because it has been skilfully repaired.

So it is in the lives of me and my daughters. We are mended pots, the more valued because of the golden seams of our rejoining, within ourselves and with each other.

The story continues; new chapters open in the books of our lives. The future is unknown. There may be another turn of the wheel, a change of direction. Growing old, for me, has been a time of change and adventure, with an increasing awareness of how we can shape our own lives by connecting with our inner energy, that 'being indoor each one dwells,' as Hopkins put it. The loneliness that Dickinson heard in the crickets' song is the loneliness of existence, of the end of summer, of separation and loss. Yet grace comes gradually through expressing our inner self and sharing with others, just as the crickets did in their unobtrusive mass.

My work as an editor continues, and writing and finishing this book brings a sense of fulfilment. Others may read this story and find resonances in their own lives. That is my wish.

Acknowledgements

As in my first two memoirs, names have been changed to protect privacy. This is a fictionalised memoir; that is, I have reconstructed remembered characters, scenes and dialogues in my earlier life from memory, using my imagination to fill in gaps. The truths contained in this story come from my heart and the understanding I have achieved of patterns in my life. This understanding has been hard-won, over many struggles and changes of direction that have brought me to a place of peace and forgiveness.

The pencil sketches were done by me.

When I published my second memoir, *A Practice of Loss*, I thought it was my last book. But many who read it told me they wanted to know more of my story, how I rebuilt my life after it was broken apart. I made a few attempts at writing this memoir and, each time, I abandoned it because it just seemed too hard to fit all the pieces together and, most of all, to write about my second marriage, which did not end in bitterness like my first, and had so many stages in our journey into separateness.

I had booked a retreat for myself in February 2022 with the intention of finishing it. So I went to the beach cabin and felt the space and peace of ocean, beach and sky, and little by little, I stitched some more pieces into the pattern and came to a point where I could see its unity. Much of the story is still silent, so it is not a long book. The pieces that have been glued together have formed a mended pot, seamed with the gold of love, containing both the spoken and the unspoken stories. The art of kintsugi brings the broken pieces together in a whole container that is more beautiful for having been broken and brought together again.

I thank Stuart Cussons, artist and sculptor, for his artwork, *Kintsugi*, that forms my cover design. The image says more than words can say, in a way that invites the reader to enter this mended space and experience the world within. Each viewer will see the kintsugi image differently, just as each reader will have their own interpretation.

For the story itself and my telling of it, my journey began when my eldest daughter (Sophia in the story) said, 'Mum, you are my mentor for writing. But you've not written anything!' So I began to write my story by hand in a school exercise book, as my mother did when I asked her to write her stories for us. Time and work intervened, and then a twist of fate made me realise that I didn't want a career, I wanted to write my story and make sense of my life. So I re-entered academia and did a Masters degree in creative writing, then went on to do a PhD in life writing. This turn in my life brought me two gifts: I found my voice in writing my life, and I became acquainted with theorists and philosophers who helped me to understand the system I was born into, and the ways that I could break free of the patterns I had inherited. So my gratitude goes to my mentors and supervisors and the wisdom they put me in touch with.

Since leaving academia and making my own pathway as a writer and an editor, I've formed many friendships and am part of professional communities of writers and editors through Facebook groups. I thank you all for your empathy and knowledge and support.

In particular, I want to thank my editor, Pamela Hewitt, who has helped me to refine the structure of this memoir and nuance some of the scenes and characters. She has been supportive and empathic and an incisive and insightful reader. It has been my best experience of having my work edited. Any flaws that remain are mine alone.

Many of my friends have encouraged me and inspired me to complete this trilogy. Thank you all.

My sincere thanks to Stephen Matthews OAM of Ginninderra Press for his patient, careful preparation of this book for publication. This is the fourth book of mine that the press has published and I am grateful for the unfailing high quality of their work.

Above all, I thank my children, my three daughters by my first marriage and my son by my second marriage. You have given my life shape and purpose and redeemed my ability to love and to have faith in life and family.

www.ingramcontent.com/pod-product-compliance
Lightning Source LLC
Chambersburg PA
CBHW070952080526
44587CB00015B/2272